BACKWARDS INTO BATTLE
A Tail Gunner's Journey
In World War II

Andy Doty

TALL TREE PRESS
OF PALO ALTO

Publisher's Note
All rights reserved. No part of this publication may be reproduced, stored in a retrieval system, or transmitted, in any form or by any means, electronic, mechanical, photocopying, recording, or otherwise, without the prior written permission of the publisher. For information address:

Tall Tree Press of Palo Alto
4072 Scripps Avenue
Palo Alto, California 94306

Telephone (415) 494-3897

Library of Congress Catalog Card Number: 95 - 090283

Copyright © Tall Tree Press of Palo Alto, 1995
ISBN 0-9646253-0-X

First Printing
Printed in the United States of America

Dedication

This book is dedicated to three crew members
of the B-29 Superfortress,
"The City of College Park"

Second Lieutenant George S. Walker, Jr.,
Navigator;

Flight officer Richard F. O'Brien,
Radar Operator;

and Master Sergeant Donald Hutchison
Flight Engineer

Who died in the final months of World War II.

Prologue

On September 2, 1945, the costliest, most destructive war in world history came to an end. The fighting had raged for six years, involved every major nation, laid waste to thousands of cities and towns, and had taken the lives of some fifty million civilians and military personnel.

More than sixteen million American men and women were in uniform. Of that number more than two million served in the Air Force — thirty-seven thousand of them as combat crew members. I was among those young airmen, a boy who grew up in a small town in upstate New York during the Great Depression, watched the war clouds gather, and eventually found himself flying twenty-one bombing missions over Japan in a B-29 Superfortress.

I have recorded my memories of that era: the impact of "hard times" and a world war on a quiet village, and the boyhood experiences of one of the last truly innocent generations of Americans. This book also traces the transition of a young man who hated fist fights into a seasoned tail gunner. Throughout my training, I was aware of what was being done to prepare me to kill or to be killed.

I think we shall never see the likes of it again. The nation was fully united and mobilized in a popular military effort. The youth of America was under arms — generally willing, and often eager, to serve their country. Young men who had never traveled more than fifteen miles from home fought land, sea, and air battles in every quarter of the globe.

Four hundred and five thousand of those servicemen died in World War II. This book is dedicated to three of those men.

Table of Contents

	Prologue	7
1	Growing Up in the Great Depression	11
2	War Comes to Hudson Falls	27
3	Into Uniform	38
4	Gunnery School	45
5	Into the Air	51
6	The B-29 Superfortress	63
7	A Crew is Formed	71
8	Into Combat	85
9	Life Between Missions	103
10	"They're Running Out of Gas"	121
11	"There is Nothing Ahead but Happiness"	128
12	Fifty Years Later	140
13	"Our Hearts Were Touched by Fire"	146
	Acknowledgments	155

Hudson Falls, New York. Dean Studio

Chapter One

Growing Up in the Great Depression

The village of Hudson Falls, N.Y. stretches for nearly two miles along the high east bank of the Hudson River, fifty miles north of the state capitol at Albany. Main Street runs parallel to the river; along its length during the 1930s were the public library, the village fire and police stations, five churches, three department stores, a bank, three drug stores, one hotel, the tiny Strand theater, the high school, the post office, and a mysterious "cigar store" where you could buy cherry bomb fireworks and where men "played the horses" in a dark, smoky poolroom in the back.

Extending east at right angles to the main thoroughfare were the usual small town streets: Maple, Elm, Willow, Chestnut. By pedaling a single-speed bike half a mile out Maple Street you could see far across the broad valley to the Green Mountains of Vermont, thirty miles away. Looking down from Main Street, you saw the wide river, tumbling along the long terrace of rocks that gave the village its name.

The city of Glens Falls lay three miles upstream, around a sweeping bend of the river. It was a major metropolis, boasting 21,000 inhabitants — three times the population of Hudson Falls. It had a downtown business district with three-story buildings, a fancy hotel, and a shiny Paramount theater. To hitch-hike or ride a bus to Glens Falls was to embark on an exciting outing.

Hudson Falls was a peaceful place. There were no serious crimes, nor scandals nor disasters to mar the slow pace of life. Snow sifted down onto the homes in the winter, lilacs bloomed beside long porches in the spring, katydids chirped on soft summer nights, and the scent of burning leaves filled the air in the fall.

The "best" part of the village was the tree-shaded streets at the center of town, at right angles to Main Street. Mechanic Street was particularly desirable. The homes of the village undertaker, the school superintendent, the banker, a department store head, and the owner of one of the three drug stores were located there. The poorer sections were at the north and south ends of town, and "under the hill," an area near the falls and the Union Bag and Paper Company mill.

Our family lived at the south end — seven of us in a large, two-story rented house. A porch ran along the front and one side. Inside were a parlor and "front room," the kitchen, dining room, and several bedrooms. The furnace stood in the center of the cellar like a huge oak, its big pipes spreading upward to the hot-air registers in the rooms above. A dark coal bin stood nearby. There was a small garden in the back of the house.

My father was a lean, angular, quiet man, proud of the fact that he had become a night shift "back-tender" on one of the paper company's big machines. He made sure that wide swaths of paper rolled smoothly through without tears or wrinkles, and he wrestled huge rolls that were half his height in diameter. He earned eighteen dollars a week and was happy to have it.

Mom was a pretty, pink-faced, somewhat disorganized woman who engaged in long, dull monologues that we learned to let slip by. She was a not a gifted cook; she would become so engrossed in reading the *Ladies Home Journal* that countless smoking dishes had to be hurriedly retrieved from the oven. Mom would scrape away the burned portion, telling her children that carbon was good for them. But she raised a large family while taking in sewing from the local shirt factory to augment Dad's income.

Three older children and a set of twins lived in the house: Bill, a taut, wiry replica of his father; Agnes, who continually drank coffee and smoked cigarettes; and Ann, as pretty as her mother. The twins — Chuck and I — came along years later — no doubt to the great dismay of their parents. Two older sisters, Betty and Ruth, had left home earlier after dropping out of school to go to work. Betty got a job in Vermont one summer, met a strong young Swede, got married, and produced a son or daughter each year on their farm for as long as I can remember. Ruth went to work in a knitting mill and rode off in an old sports car to marry a carefree fellow named Neil Norton.

Chuck and I were fraternal twins — brothers who happened to be born at the same time, October 12, 1925. We turned out to be quite different. I did all the "right" things: finished my chores, studied hard in school, and earned Boy Scout merit badges. In high school I played on four sports teams, portrayed Editor Webb in *Our Town*, and was named president of our senior class. I was the fair-haired son, and knew it — something I still feel guilty about. Chuck marched to his own drummer. He was taller and stronger than I, but he cared little about sports. He was self-taught in many ways; I was amazed by the store of information he acquired about nature, animals, electricity, and many other subjects. He quietly handled the lighting and other electrical details of our high school drama productions.

It was not at all unusual that my older brother and sisters had dropped out of school early. The vast majority of Depression-era children did not proceed beyond eighth grade, for they had to work or marry to ease the economic burden on their families. Agnes proudly showed us the razor-sharp, crescent-shaped blade attached to a ring that she wore on her finger while working on a production line at the paper company. Her job was to bundle paper bags as rapidly as she could. She tied up the batches, then cut the cord with a sweep of her razor, losing little time in the process. Ann, Chuck and I were the lucky ones in the family; we were able to continue into high school, thanks to our older brother and sisters.

The Howe family lived nearby. The ages of the children in the two families dovetailed nicely. Bill married Leah Howe, a teacher in a local school, and Agnes married Ken, a foreman who worked in the paper mill at Fenimore, on the other side of the Hudson River. Ann and young Frank Howe were "seeing each other" quite seriously before he tripped on a coil of rope at the mill one night and plunged through an opening to his death on the concrete floor below. Warning signs, barricades, proper lighting, hard hats and other safety measures were luxuries in those days. The company was not seen as liable in any way, so no thought was given to possible legal action.

A tragic accident had occurred, but that's the way things were.

In much the same way, bus riders on their way to Glens Falls had to hold their noses as their vehicle passed through a cloud of sulfurous, rotten-egg down-wash from a nearby cement plant. The fallout covered a cluster of wretched downwind houses with a layer of yellow film. But that was simply the unfortunate, and unquestioned, by-product of the plant. And of course the poor people who lived in the houses paid low rents. America's environmental awareness stood then where that of eastern Europe stands today.

Our family was poor, but lucky to have jobs. Forty million Americans had no work or regular income in the mid-1930s, and unemployment ran as high as 80% in some cities. Fortunately, the paper products of the mills were in demand. Dad worked six days a week, and Mom sewed when she was not cleaning, washing or scorching dinner. We had no car, no telephone, no family vacations, and no bicycles for many years (the Montgomery Ward model cost a staggering $29). I have a clear memory of dinners consisting of a slice of bread in a soup plate, covered with milk and sprinkled with sugar. At one time we ate dandelion greens that Dad dug up from a field. We complained about the bitterness, but were told that the greens, like charred cake, would make us strong. We needed only to add some butter and salt.

Doctors were too expensive for casual use. One winter night I was sliding down a hill at the same time a girl was pulling her Flexible Flyer sled up the slope. The sled was behind her, trailing at the end of a long rope. Without her realizing it, the sled strayed out into my path. I was flat on my stomach, hands extended out to the steering handles as I sped down the hill. There was no time or room to turn. I smashed into her sled, the bridge of my nose catching the steel frame at the front. I rolled off my sled as blood spilled onto the snow. My companions placed me on the sled and pulled me home, where my mother applied her favorite remedy, a "cold poultice" — a bandage soaked in cold water. No doctor was called, nor did we ever visit one. I still bear the scar and skewed nose.

Chuck and I asked Dad for a dime apiece one Saturday to attend the afternoon matinee at the Strand. "I just don't have it, boys," he said, and turned his pockets inside-out to show us. Although disappointed, I felt an even deeper sadness for him. Waitresses were averaging $520 a year in income, construction workers $900, textile workers $435, and secretaries, $1,000. Wages were routinely reduced at the same time work weeks were extended, and no one dared complain. In fact, Dad had been "let go" from an earlier paper mill job in another town when he dared talk about the need for a worker's union.

Christmas brought few gifts. Chuck and I could expect a new penknife each year from Betty, knitted mittens (with our initials on the cuffs) from maiden Aunt Gertrude, and an article of clothing or two and a home-made toy from Mom and Dad.

The announcer during the "Fibber Magee and Molly" radio show would tantalize us with his descriptions of Mars candy bars. He spoke in slow, mellow tones of the "rich, creamy caramel," the "crunchy almonds," and the "smooth chocolate" that made up candy we could not afford. As we walked the sidewalks of Hudson Falls our eyes scanned the pavement ahead, searching for lost coins. A penny was great, a nickel was a real find, and a quarter would send the finder into ecstasy. I dreamed of finding that much money.

The Delaware and Hudson railroad tracks were not far from our house. My father called the D & H the "Delay and Halt," but it did succeed in carrying some of that era's one million homeless — men called hoboes — into northern New York. They stole rides in railroad boxcars, cooked food in tin cans over wood fires, and slept in "jungles" in the woods. They chalked secret codes onto village curbs and sidewalks to direct others to hospitable homes — or to warn them away from unfriendly ones. Some made their way to our house, where my mother gave them a slice of bread and butter when it was available. They were courteous, grateful, and subdued as they sat on our back steps. Chuck and I stole glances at their bearded faces, grimy clothes and worn shoes.

"Where are you from?" we asked one.

"From all over. You name it, I bin there."

"Where you going?"

"Wherever I can catch onta something."

When we were able to go to the theater, we watched the Fox Movietone News coverage of bloody strikes in automobile and steel factories. There were other scenes of men in black overcoats standing stoically in block-long bread lines, and of former executives selling apples, pencils and shoestrings from tiny sidewalk stands. There were dirty, seamed "Okies" fleeing the dust storms that had overwhelmed their farms. We saw an army of World War I veterans march on Washington to demand early payment of bonuses due them in 1945. Those were "hard times" indeed.

A new president came into office, his cigarette holder cocked at a jaunty angle, and announced a "New Deal" of relief, recovery, and reform to lift the nation out of the Depression. Among Franklin Roosevelt's programs was the WPA (Works Projects Administration). It created jobs for the unemployed all over America. An empty corner lot near our house that lacked sidewalks and curbs was targeted for improvement. One day a truck and a dozen men arrived, hammered a WPA sign into the ground, and began shoveling. They worked leisurely that summer, stretching out the job as long as possible.

My father and brother Bill, establishing their own pecking order, looked down upon the slow-moving workers across the street.

"Do you know why the WPA needs a crew of eight and a portable out-house to hoe a field that two men can handle?" my father would ask with a slight smile. "Because there are always two coming, two going, two peeing, and two hoeing."

Our village was the perfect place for boyhood. The river, vacant lots, and nearby ponds and wooded areas were our playgrounds. Our school classes were small, and our summer vacations were delicious. Our "gang" of boys — far different from the city thugs of today — hiked across a bridge to roam the wooded Fenimore banks, named after James Fenimore Cooper, whose *Last of the Mohicans* was set in our area. We tried to run silently along paths through the trees and walk with our toes pointed straight ahead, as we were told the Indians once did. We swam naked in the river at a remote shale beach. An old row boat washed up onto the shore after a storm; we lugged it home, where we replaced broken bottom boards, pounded rope into the cracks, and sealed it all with chunks of tar melted in a tin can over a small fire. We paddled about happily on sunny afternoons in our resurrected craft.

We entertained ourselves in many ways: by building, defending, and storming snow forts in the winter, by racing match-sticks down a street gutter in the spring run-off, or by nudging a small wheel along the street with a T-shaped device we had hammered together. A kite could be built from strips of wood, string, newspaper, some paste, and a tail of torn rags. It was serviceable and was no great loss when it tangled inevitably in a tree or telephone lines.

The seasons dictated our activities: football in the fall, ice hockey and basketball in the winter, baseball and track in the spring. Sprung free from school in June like colts turned out to pasture, we went swimming in the river and fished for slippery, long-whiskered "bullheads." My father told us his favorite recipe for preparing river carp.

"You put the carp on a board, bake it in an oven for an hour, pull it out, throw the carp away, and eat the board."

There were many empty lots in town. Riding two-on-a-bike and carrying a scruffy football, we challenged other gangs to Saturday morning battles. We tangled in the dust and mud without benefit of Pop Warner League helmets, padding or cleated shoes. There were no obnoxious "high-fives" nor show-off victory dances after a touchdown. Not a coach nor a parent was in sight.

We believed our gang to be unique. "McGoosey" Walsh was a freckled imp who could drop two-handed set shots into a hoop almost at will. Bob Burns was a skinny Irishman. He was a choir boy in the Catholic church, but was far from angelic. Bob could swear with the best of us, but he could go to confession on Saturday to be absolved of his guilt. As a Methodist, I envied the protection he gained by dipping his fingers into the water to cross himself before we went swimming or before he took a foul shot in basketball. Later in life I wondered if a controlled experiment would show that Catholics who crossed themselves drowned less often or made more foul shots than Methodists who did not.

Bill DeCamillo could not look more Italian than he did. So we called him "Irish Bill." Later on, in high school, he affected a "zoot suit." He wore a bright yellow, absurdly long jacket. His lavender pegged pants, supported by bright suspenders, reached up to his rib cage. A key chain drooped nearly to the ankles. His wide-brimmed fedora hat would have done justice to a Chicago gangster. His were the first male fingernails I ever saw that were an inch long.

"Bud" Reed was devilishly inventive. One dark night, as we were liberating apples from someone's backyard trees, the owner heard us, turned on a light, and looked out the door. As we ran away, Bud called back:

"Get down out of that tree, Mark LaRue, son of Reverend LaRue." Mark was a popular boy who of course was not with us. The next day, his kindly father received a phone call from the angry owner.

Although we grew up in a small village and came from humble stock, we were surprisingly literate. We prided ourselves on the nicknames we devised for village characters: "Shuffle-foot" Gleason, "Choo-Choo" Trayne, "Carstairs" Lethbridge (after his favorite whiskey) and "Commodore" Logan. The Commodore was tall, handsome and distinguished in his cast-off clothing. He had no job, and, as far as we could tell, no home. He was allowed to sleep at night in a barber shop chair or in the back of Harry Baker's Square Deal Drugstore.

We also were pleased with the store of limericks we had memorized. Our favorite was "The Man From Pawnee":

> There once was a man from Pawnee
> Who made love to an ape in a tree.
> The result was *most* horrid,
> All ass and no forehead,
> *Three* balls and a purple goatee.

We recited it in unison, with appropriate emphasis and gestures. We illustrated "an ape in a tree" by pointing upward, and "all ass" by shaping large, round curves. As we said "no forehead," we passed our hands across our brows. "Three balls" called for three fingers held upright. For the final phrase, "and a purple goatee," we stroked our chins. The exercise never failed to delight us.

Our days were enlivened by the arrival on our street of the ice man, the rag man and the vegetable man. Their coming was announced by loud calls, bells, or whistles. The ice man's truck was piled high with large, clear blocks covered by bits of sawdust and wet canvas. He snagged the blocks down with his tongs, chipped them to the right size, hoisted them onto a leather patch on his shoulder, and bore them to the ice boxes in our homes. While he was away, we sucked on the ice shards on hot summer days.

The rag man was a shrewd old fellow who offered a few coins for all the cloth and scrap metal we could collect. "Rags, rags, rags," he called, and we dragged to his truck a burlap bag half filled with rusted nuts and bolts we had dug up from the Sandy Hill Iron and Brass Company yard. He was engaged in recycling long before the word was invented.

A ringing bell told us when the vegetable man was in our neighborhood. His wares were displayed on slanted racks in the back of his truck, shaded by an awning. A scooped scale dangled from a chain. Our mothers came out, wiping their hands on their aprons, to select from the fruits and vegetables when they could afford them.

As soon as we could, we found jobs. Three of us weeded Mr. Bushbaum's yard and garden at fifteen cents each for the full Saturday morning. Ten cents got us into the afternoon movie, leaving five cents for candy. "Vaht robbers!" he roared one day when we gathered the courage to ask him for twenty cents a morning. We did not pursue it further; his was a buyer's market.

At age fifteen, Bob Burns, McGoosey, Chuck, and I obtained our working papers and began caddying at the Glens Falls Country Club. After two years we worked our way up to the highest "Double A" status. That qualified us to advise golfers on which clubs to use, and to carry a heavy golf bag on each shoulder for thirty-six to forty-five holes on a good day. If we were polite, quickly handed out the proper clubs, and complimented our clients for their solid shots, we could expect a modest tip. As we trudged up and down the hills on those summer days the voices of the Andrews Sisters carried across a lake from a pavilion loudspeaker. They sang "I'll Be With You in Apple Blossom Time," and "Bei Mir Bist Du Schon," and my heart sang with them. We were young, healthy, outdoors, and earning money.

Between rounds, we sometimes walked through the pine woods to the tenth hole, where we hid in the low-hanging branches, over a hill from the tee. As the golfers' drives came bounding over we dashed out, picked up the balls, and threw them far down the fairway. Back in the trees, we laughed as the resplendent bankers, doctors, dentists, and lawyers marveled at how far they had driven their balls. What wonderful clubhouse stories must have followed.

One summer I saved a total of fifty-two dollars. With it, I bought a pair of Thom McAn shoes, gabardine pants, a sport coat — and had a bit left over. During the winter, some of us set up pins at a bowling alley for thirty cents a "string," or $1.10 on a good night. Automatic pin-setters had yet to be invented, so we stood in the corner of the pit, braced our arms on the back and side, and flung our legs high in the air as the ball sent the pins flying. Failure to swing high enough could result in some painful bruises. Then we picked up the pins, two crossed necks in each hand, and stood them back up, four at a time. We loved gutter balls, for they required no work nor gymnastics.

My hobbies taught me to be patient, and that I was comfortable when I was alone — a characteristic that would serve me well later on. I spent hours in a warm basement retreat I had set up next to the furnace, where a bare light bulb hung over a card table. I worked on my stamp collection, purchased with earnings from pin-setting. Fat bags of canceled stamps arrived from New York and I excitedly dumped them onto my table. No prospector ever combed through dirt more thoroughly than I searched those gummed bits from around the world. Most of them were prosaic English queens, German castles, and French fleurs-de-lis, but now and then a marvelous triangular from Mongolia or an octagonal from Uruguay would be discovered, to be pasted into my book with little slips of translucent adhesive paper. Madagascar, Liechtenstein and Estonia became real places through that exercise.

My friends and I were caught up in building model airplanes and in identifying aircraft of all kinds. We knew the name of virtually every plane in the world, ranging from tiny American Gee Bee racers to giant Italian Caproni bombers. Balsawood kits could be purchased for fifteen to twenty-five cents. The models were built from scratch: ribs cut out with a razor blade; stringers glued into notches with airplane cement to form the fuselage; wings and tails assembled, covered with tissue paper, and attached. A World War I Spad, a Sopwith Camel and a tri-winged Fokker took shape on my table, as did a Piper Cub, a Seversky P-35 and a Gloster Gauntlet biplane. The Gauntlet cost a dollar, my most expensive purchase. Tears came to my eyes the night an entire wing burst into flame when I held it too close to the stove to make the doped skin tight enough to impress my friends. It took hours to reconstruct from surplus balsa.

Our school teachers were dedicated women, mostly unmarried, who demanded that we diagram the structure of sentences properly, recite the multiplication tables without a slip, and remember the outcome of the Peloponnesian Wars. Their right to grab an unruly boy by the ear and hustle him out the door and into the principal's office was unquestioned.

I fell in love with words and rhymes at an early age. I was fascinated by adjectives and looked for the rhyming patterns in *The Ancient Mariner*, *Hiawatha*, *Lochinvar*, *The Highwayman*, and *Paul Revere's Ride*. I often found myself thinking in rhymes.

An early hero of mine was Horatius, from *Horatius at the Gate*.

"Then up spake brave Horatius,
Captain of the Gate,

> To every man upon this earth,
> Death cometh soon or late."

The young Roman strode out with his sword to hold off the enemy until his companions destroyed the bridge behind him. Then he swam the Tiber to safety. I admired his sturdy courage.

The Merchant of Venice touched me, as did Millet's painting of "The Man With a Hoe." There is a sad, hopeless look in that weary peasant's face that I found unforgettable. Could it be that I saw in him my own vacation-less father and siblings who had disappeared into the mills? Or did I see my own future as an unskilled laborer? I did not know what else I could do.

I was filled with the ambivalence of youth: quite confident at times, but insecure and uncertain at others; sometimes terribly shy, but pleased by attention; gregarious, yet often preferring to be alone; able to lead, but quite willing to follow.

I dreaded the fist fights that broke out after school or during our sandlot games. Honor required a boy to fight when challenged, so I often found myself taking a longer route home from school to avoid one thug in particular whose major reason for attending class seemed to be to pick fights afterward. There was a chip on his shoulder at all times. It actually came to that. He would place a bit of wood there and dare another boy to knock it off. Of course the other had to; great loss of face would result if he did not. Then the scuffle would begin, starting with wildly swung fists and invariably ending up with the two grappling in the dirt or snow — one, if not both, hoping all the while that they would be broken apart by their friends or a teacher or a mother who happened on the scene.

Although our gang engaged in pranks, stole apples from trees, and later found ways to sneak into the Strand theater without paying, we were among the last truly innocent generations in America. We did not drink or smoke, or gamble. Drugs were unheard of, except for the rumor that certain big band drummers used something called marijuana. We did not swear in front of girls or insult them in any way. When an opponent took his foul shots in a basketball game, fans and players alike remained silent and unmoving so as not to disturb him.

We fought fair. Two boys never picked on one, nor one boy on a smaller opponent. Kicking was not tolerated. Anyone caught carrying a knife was subject to permanent banishment. Firearms were totally out of the question.

Over the years our attention shifted from bicycles and ice skates to how we combed our hair, to our clothing, to shaving — to girls. We watched the movie actors shave — men lathering, screwing up their faces, tugging at a cheek with one hand as the other drew a broad razor through the thick, white cream. We timidly roller-skated with girls to organ music at Brennan's Roller Rink on the Lake George highway, hands sweating and minds groping for a few words of conversation. There were later games of "Spin-the-Bottle" and "Post Office," with chaste kisses at stake.

We knew next to nothing about sex, even though some of our high school classmates told us they were experts on the subject. Our parents avoided the topic and our schools taught us little. The movies were discreet, songs were discreet, magazines were discreet. The most salacious material available to us was the silk stocking ads in the Montgomery Ward catalog. Hand-holding and kissing were allowed after several dates with a girl, but a boy did not try to go "too far" if he really cared for her. Parental wrath, peer disapproval among the girls and the fear of pregnancy hung over our era.

A carnival visited Hudson Falls for a week every summer and I could feel the excitement spread throughout town. Admission was free, so we roamed the brightly-lighted, sawdust-covered grounds every night. We watched "death-defying" motorcyclists rev up their machines before entering a fat silo to roar horizontally within its high walls. There were games of chance where a ball rolled down a chute onto a fenced-in field of cupcake tins, each cup painted a different color. For a nickel you could try to guess the color of the cup in which the ball would come to rest, thereby winning a handful of nickels — which invariably were reinvested until they were all gone. A woman with long black hair sat in a two-piece bathing suit in a canvas pit, playing with a large snake that curled over her shoulders as others slithered about her feet.

But best of all — the event that sent us racing across the grounds from wherever we were — was the "hootchee-kootchee" show. Loud drums and a barker's voice drew us to the scene of the next performance. BOOM- boom- boom, BOOM- boom- boom, BOOM-boom-boom, sounded the drums.

"Right over here, right over here, come on over here," called the barker. "Come see this little lady jiggle and jounce. She's got what it takes and wants ta prove it. Com'n right up, don't be shy, come right up."

We took him at his word and crowded to the edge of the outdoor stage. The barker looked down on us with disdain. "Get outa here, you little squirts," he said with a wave of his hand. "G'wan home and get to bed." But we stayed to look up at a girl in a frayed rayon wrap-around. Her face was expressionless as she shuffled a few steps back and forth in time with the drum. As she did the wrap would part, revealing bare legs. We could not afford the admission fee, but were told that for twenty-five cents she would take off most of her clothes and for another twenty-five she would show all.

One day when we were quite young, three of us hitch-hiked home from Glens Falls. A car containing two youths and a young woman stopped to pick us up. We crowded into the back seat. The girl sat between the men in the front. We had heard of her; she was quite mature and had a reputation for being "fast." As we drove along, she played her audience perfectly. She inhaled her cigarette, slowly blew out the smoke, and turned to one of the men.

"Did you remember to bring the raincoats?" she asked.

"Right here," he said, touching his pocket.

"I think we're going to need them," she said.

We were flabbergasted. We knew what she was talking about — "rubbers," the 1930s name for condoms. Our eyes widened and we tilted each other sideways with our nudges. We could hardly wait to get back to tell the rest of the gang about what we had heard.

Many years later we learned that a member of our class, Prom Queen Peg McGinnis, had been even more innocent. She was working in Moriarty's drug store one night when a man entered and asked if he could buy some rubbers.

"I'm sorry, we don't have any," she answered. "But Heil's shoe store is just down the block. You might try them." Afterward, Mr. Moriarty quietly came forward to suggest that she refer all such future inquiries to him.

Not everyone in our high school was innocent, to be sure. One fat senior — the counterpart of today's drug pusher — was known as the "rubber man" for the items he sold covertly to a few custom-

Northeastern New York Conference Champions, 1943. The author is player number 10.

ers. Another member of our football team warned his Ft. Ann girl friend that her sexual parts would "grow shut" if she failed to accommodate him. But in general, we could only wonder what it was all about.

Sports brought many rewards. I was not big, but could run fast and far. During my high school years I ran the mile in track, played guard on the basketball team and second base on the baseball team. The eleven starters on our football squad played the full game, on offense and defense. When we had the ball I was a halfback in an old single-wing attack that featured reverses and plunges off a straight snap from the center. On defense I was the deep safety and returned punts.

We called our coach the "Genial Mentor." Elmer Heidorf was a former Fordham lineman who taught elementary, secondary and high school physical education during the day and coached the junior varsity and varsity squads after school. He oversaw three sports and handled team scheduling, team discipline and gym floor re-waxing with aplomb. He wore the same warm-up uniform every day, had no assistants, and sold basketball shoes on the side from his tiny office overlooking our tiny gymnasium.

Main Street in Hudson Falls. Dean Studio

We received only rudimentary football training, had a slender play book, and did not confuse our opponents with a sophisticated offense. The team photo shows uniforms that did not match perfectly and helmets without face masks. Nevertheless, we were a good, solid team, and went undefeated in my senior year. We beat the fearsome Golden Horde of Granville in a War Bond benefit playoff game before a monster crowd of 2,100 at Derby Field — with most of the fans standing along the sidelines. "Tex" Bailey, the owner of a village saloon, bet an astronomical fifty dollars on the game, an unheard-of amount in those days. He happily pummeled us all the way back to our tiny, cement-block locker room.

The summer before that final season Bob Burns and I went to work at the Imperial Paint and Paper Company in Glens Falls. We were assigned to the yard gang, where we unloaded by hand railroad box-cars filled with knee-high stacks of cement bags that weighed one hundred pounds apiece. We stood on a high platform in the oppressive heat and fumes, shoveling heavy, tinsel-like shreds of lead into wide vats of acid as the metal dropped relentlessly from a conveyor belt onto a steel plate. We pushed carts of crushed ice up to the paint-mixers — men whose hats, overalls, shoes, faces, and hands were red, green, blue or yellow. They must have sweated primary colors.

It was at the Imperial that the name of Eleanor Baker, daughter of the Mechanic Street pharmacist, first came to my attention. A fellow worker from Glens Falls said he had noticed her and thought she was "cute." Had I ever thought of dating her? I had not. Her family was high on the Hudson Falls social ladder, while ours was out of sight on the rungs below.

But the seed was planted. Eleanor sat in front of me in history class that Fall and I finally worked up the courage to ask her to go on a hayride. She accepted and other dates followed. She was pretty, poised, intelligent, and totally unpretentious. Freshly washed, light brown hair fell to her shoulders. She wore soft, baggy sweaters, a pearl necklace, pleated plaid skirts, bobby sox, and saddle shoes. I was hooked. The day after our first date, I dramatically announced to my teammates that I had found the girl I would marry some day.

Life was good that fall of 1943, except for one thing: the guns of war had been rumbling over the horizon during most of my boyhood, and the sound was coming closer.

CHAPTER TWO
WAR COMES TO HUDSON FALLS

Hardly a week passed during the 1930s when our school *Weekly Reader*, the Glens Falls *Post Star*, or *LIFE Magazine* failed to carry news of some far-off conflict. Aggressors were on the march and little stood in their way.

Japan invaded Manchuria and China, Italy subdued Ethiopia, and the Spanish Civil War ran its cruel course. We were shocked by a LIFE photograph of a naked Chinese baby crying in bombed ruins, by the Japanese rape of Nanking, and by photos of Nipponese soldiers bayoneting and beheading bound Chinese prisoners. An Italian pilot — the son of Dictator Benito Mussolini — casually observed that when his bombs exploded among Ethiopian natives, a "beautiful" pattern resulted that reminded him of the petals of a flower slowly unfolding.

Hitler came to power in Germany and began building one of the most formidable military machines in history. He annexed Austria in 1938, then demanded that Czechoslovakia's Sudetenland be turned over to Germany. Even a thirteen-year-old boy could see war coming to Europe. The major nations made no secret of the fact they had tested their weapons in Spain's Civil War, and Hitler's appetite seemed insatiable.

"Ye shall hear of wars, and rumors of war," my father told us fatalistically, quoting from the Bible. Although Matthew went on to say "see that ye not be troubled: for all these things must come to pass, but the end is not yet," I understood Dad to mean that war was an inevitable fact of life. I could see no reason to disagree.

Later in 1938, Prime Minister Neville Chamberlain of England returned from a meeting with Hitler in Munich, smiling as he waved a signed agreement he declared had won "peace in our time." Chamberlain had given Hitler the land he wanted, over the protests of the Czechs. A year later, the German dictator scrapped the agreement and occupied the rest of the country.

World War II broke out on September 1, 1939, after Germany invaded Poland. England and France, finally realizing that appeasement had failed, declared war. Poland fell in a matter of days, the victim of swift Panzer tank divisions and Stuka dive-bombers.

A long lull — "the Phony War" — followed, during which little fighting occurred. America debated whether or not to take sides. My youthful sympathies clearly laid with England and France, but the memory of World War I was still fresh in the minds of older, wiser men and women. "What did we get from the first world war but death, debt, and George M. Cohan?" the isolationists asked. Their cries of "Never Again" and "America First" held strong appeal. Congress passed yet another Neutrality Act as public opinion polls in December of 1939 showed more than two-thirds of the people opposed involvement in Europe's problems.

An amazing reversal took place during the next six months. German troops occupied Denmark and Norway in April of 1940, paused, then swept across the Netherlands, Belgium, Luxembourg and northern France in a devastating "Blitzkrieg" attack. After only ten days of battle, Hitler stood on the shores of the English Channel. Newsreels showed long lines of British troops at Dunkirk, farther to the west, waiting to be evacuated by a flotilla of every English naval or pleasure craft that could cross over to France. England was standing alone, and a surge of pro-British feelings resulted. A survey that May revealed a dramatic shift in public opinion: more than two-thirds of Americans favored active aid to England.

Shortly afterward, Congress passed the Selective Service Act of 1940, and the nation began arming itself. In the next two years, the Army grew from a force of 190,000 men to 1.5 million. Isolationism had been a persuasive force, but it gave way to America's instinctive support of freedom and democracy. The feeling slowly grew that England had to be saved and Hitler defeated.

Photos began to appear of raw recruits at the Plattsburg Army base practicing with wooden cannon, or with trucks bearing signs that read "Tank." Real equipment was not yet available in any great number. In Glens Falls, a hotel was taken over to house fledgling aviation cadets. We saw the uniformed young men marching to their pre-flight classes on the way to becoming pilots, navigators, and bombardiers.

The "Battle of Britain" swirled over England that summer. To pave the way for an invasion of the island, Hitler sent out his bombers to hit military targets and destroy the Royal Air Force. After suffering heavy losses — and not knowing that his Luftwaffe had worn the RAF down to its last reserve squadrons — he changed tactics and ordered the blanket nighttime bombing of London and other cities. That shift saved the RAF. London could absorb the terrible punishment, but the RAF could not have fought much longer.

"This.... is London," was Edward R. Murrow's dramatic introduction of his nightly radio broadcasts. We listened as Londoners huddled in deep underground shelters, bombs erupted, and smoke shrouded St. Paul's Cathedral. But Hitler had missed his chance to invade England after Dunkirk, and failed to subdue England through bombing. He called off the invasion, and turned his armies and air force south and east in 1941 to attack North Africa, Yugoslavia, Greece, Crete, and the Soviet Union. Britain drew a sigh of relief.

One Sunday afternoon in December of 1941, Chuck and I came into the house to find our parents close to the radio.

"The losses have been heavy," the announcer was saying.

"What's happening?" we asked.

"The Japs have bombed Pearl Harbor," my father said quietly. "They sneaked in this morning. We're going to have to fight them."

Living in the East and watching Europe, we had not been following events in the Pacific as closely. The United States opposed Japan's expansion into Southeast Asia and had embargoed oil, steel and scrap metal shipments to that nation. Japan struck back while it was strong and America weak. What made the attack even more despicable in our minds was the fact that Japanese emissaries were in Washington to negotiate peace at the same time their aircraft carriers were slipping across the Pacific toward Hawaii.

The grim reports continued throughout that day and the next. Eight battleships and three cruisers had been sunk or damaged, 188 airplanes were destroyed, and 2,400 men had been killed. The next day, newspapers showed sunken battleships at their berths, damaged buildings, and the smoldering ruins of airplanes on the ground. It had been a devastating blow.

December 7, 1941, branded by President Roosevelt as "the day that will live in infamy," propelled the United States into war against both Japan and its allies, Germany and Italy.

I did not feel great concern at the time. Hawaii was far away and we had faith in our nation's ability to recover. A commonly held view was that the Japanese were poor fighters, possessed inferior equipment, and could be "licked" in a matter of months. We took satisfaction in a popular story that the Japanese once faithfully copied the stolen design of a English battleship, not realizing that the plans had deliberately been altered to make the ship top-heavy. When the ship was launched it promptly turned turtle, and floated bottom-up in the water — or so the story went.

The years pass by slowly at age sixteen, so it seemed possible that the war could be fought and won before Chuck and I reached draft age in October of 1943. If not, we would serve without question. We had to do our duty: the nation must be defended, and Pearl Harbor had to be avenged. We drifted slowly toward the vortex as the months passed.

Red, white and blue service flags began to appear in the front windows of village homes, a star for each son in uniform. In time the village was drained of virtually all of its able-bodied men between the ages of eighteen and thirty-six. Everyone was expected to take up arms, and those who did not — the physically unfit "4-Fs" and those in essential occupations — were looked down upon. "Draft-dodger" and "slacker" were bitter epithets.

"Why aren't you in uniform?" older adults demanded of young men who appeared to be of service age. The question could have stemmed from patriotism or jealousy, or both.

"They're either too young or too old," actress Bette Davis sang in a movie, referring to those who remained behind. "They're either too gray or too grassy green... What's good is in the Army, what's left can never harm me."

McGoosey Walsh quit school to join the Navy, where he became a radio operator on a submarine in the Pacific. Bob Burns' brother Ed entered an officer's training program at Rensselaer Polytechnic Institute and became a naval gunnery officer. My older cousin, a plumber by trade, was assigned to duty as a mechanic in a P-47 fighter squadron. Eleanor Baker's brother entered an Army officer candidate's school. Hudson Falls High School's music director was stationed in Washington, where he led a Marine Corps band and returned home often on leave, resplendent in full dress uniform.

In time, gold stars that symbolized lost sons, husbands and fathers began to replace service flags. Chuck Eagle, the center on our football team, worked at night behind the soda fountain at Moriarty's Drug Store. The store also housed a Western Union office. When telegrams from the War Department arrived, it was Chuck's duty to deliver them to village homes after work. Mothers and wives fearfully opened their doors to him those nights. "The Secretary of War desires me to express his deep regret," the telegrams began, that your son or husband has been killed or wounded, or is missing in action. The telegrams seemed to arrive far too often. Chuck hated the task. A total of 126 young men from our sparsely-populated county were killed in the war, two dozen of them from Hudson Falls. Untold numbers were wounded or captured.

The wounded began drifting back. Pat DuPell, the big, strong, red-haired brother of one of our gang members, came home from the Navy badly scarred, nearly blind, and breathing through an opening in his throat. A depot of depth charges had exploded next to his barracks at an eastern naval base. We were shocked by his appearance. Word came back that Chuck LaFountain, a bright young classmate who had entered the Army Air Force before his graduation, had been killed in the crash of an experimental aircraft called a flying wing.

At the Sandy Hill Iron and Brass Works, machinists began making base plates for machine guns, then turned out heavy winches for landing ships. The firm proudly floated a Navy "E" for Excellence pennant from its flagpole. Married and too old to be drafted, my brother Bill left the paper mill to spray paint the heavy tanks coming off a new assembly line at the American Locomotive Works in Schenectady.

Meat, coffee, butter, cheese, sugar, flour and other foods became scarce. Our parents took their ration books of stamps to the stores, "spending" points for a pound of butter or a slice of ham. Gas was rationed, as well. An "A" card allowed the owner three gallons a week. A "B" card enabled a driver to obtain a few more gallons if truly needed. The "X" card was granted those in essential enterprises.

Bill obtained one for his daily trips with other workers to the tank factory. At night, Chuck Eagle would take his father's car out to drain any remaining drops from gas pump hoses at closed stations.

Hudson Falls High School canceled all track meets to conserve gas, but the baseball season went on. There were games in nearby Glens Falls and Ft. Edward. Jim Fraser and I preferred track over baseball, so we memorized a poem:

"Oh, for the days of the track team, the track team.

Oh, for the days of the cinder path.

Oh, for the days of the hurdle, the high jump.

Oh, for the days of the hundred yard dash."

We thought we were quite clever, and chanted the verse in the rear of the bus as we returned from baseball games. If our coach, the Genial Mentor, heard us from his seat up front next to the driver, he never let on— much less comment on the poor rhyming.

A collection center for items vital to the war effort was set up near the fire station. Villagers brought in scrap metal, vegetable fats, empty toothpaste tubes, rubber tires, metal foil, silk stockings, flattened tin cans and waste paper. "Lucky Strike Green Has Gone to War!" a cigarette company proudly proclaimed. I assumed that it was doing its part by abandoning the use of scarce tin foil in its packages.

Victory gardens sprouted; war bond drives were mounted; women wrapped bandages; older men volunteered to be air raid wardens. Wearing armbands and helmets and holding a page of silhouettes of German bombers, the wardens stood ready in case the Luftwaffe targeted Hudson Falls.

The saddest hours of the war occurred during the spring of 1942. The Axis powers — Germany, Italy and Japan — were invincible. Their armies were spread across Europe, were approaching Egypt and Moscow, and ranged in the Pacific from Burma south to New Guinea, east to the Gilbert Islands, and north to the Aleutians. Axis navies were in command of the high seas. German submarines torpedoed American tankers within sight of the East Coast and America's old P-40 and P-39 fighter planes fell quickly before Japan's excellent new Zero. So much for the belief that the Japanese could only copy designs developed by others.

Nevertheless, it was inconceivable to me that "our side" could lose. I was certain that someday, somehow, the Axis armies and navies would be halted and thrown back.

The tide slowly began to turn soon afterward. Japan's mighty fleet of aircraft carriers — the same ships that had launched the planes to attack Pearl Harbor the previous December — was defeated in June at the Battle of Midway. British troops routed Rommel's Afrika Corps in the Libyan desert and sent it reeling back toward Tunisia. The Soviets halted the Germans at Stalingrad after a ferocious struggle. American troops landed in Algeria. The long, hard, costly march to Berlin, Rome and Tokyo had begun. We traced the movement of the allied forces on newspaper maps, unaware that the salients and advancing lines on those pieces of paper were made at a cost of thousands of dead or wounded young men. Once again, Chuck and I thought the war might be over by the time we reached our eighteenth birthdays on October 12, 1943.

It wasn't.

When that date arrived, the *New York Times* reported that the American Fifth Army, after making its way across North Africa, through Sicily and into Italy, was inching toward Rome against fierce German resistance, hampered by rain, mud and flood waters. Our Eighth Air Force in England was flying raids deep into Germany that were so costly in men and machines they had to be suspended, although that was not announced at the time. One mission, mounted against the ball-bearing factory at Schweinfurt, Germany two days after my birthday, resulted in a loss of 60 aircraft out of the 291 that participated.

In the Pacific theater, other American troops were fighting the Japanese in the jungles of New Georgia. "Long Pacific War Ahead, Says Flier," read one headline.

That week's issue of *LIFE Magazine* contained photos of American troops recapturing Attu in the Aleutians, of Australian infantry being landed at Lae in New Guina, and a story about a B-17 bomber that crash-landed in England after a mission to Stuttgart.

The advertisements in the magazine illustrated "How To Jockey a General Sherman" (tank), how Parker Quink with Solv-X spared rubber and metal parts, and how the use of Pennzoil would save gas for the war effort. The cover of the next week's issue showed a young soldier sadly bidding farewell to his new bride.

I registered for the draft after my birthday, ready to enter the service when I completed high school in January. There was no way of knowing at the time, but that delay of three months — from my birthday to my January graduation — later was to play quite an important part in my life.

The three months passed swiftly. I had been taking "commercial" courses in high school rather than college-entrance subjects because I had no hope of attending a university. In the fall of 1943, I enrolled in classes in math and physics in the hope they would better prepare me for one of the armed forces. On weekend evenings, Eleanor Baker taught me dance steps at parties in homes with the rugs rolled up. I clumsily fox-trotted to "People Will Say We're in Love" and haltingly jitterbugged to Glenn Miller's "String of Pearls" and Tommy Dorsey's "Boogie Woogie." By November, we had agreed to "go steady."

Invited to lunch at the Baker home on Mechanic Street, I noticed that Eleanor's mother and older sister sliced their sandwiches on the diagonal. Our family cut them straight across the middle. It was clear to me that we had been doing it the wrong way all those years. That simple, elegant cut symbolized the difference between the lower middle class and the upper middle class in Hudson Falls.

Our football team began a five-game schedule against local schools. I ascribed unique strengths to each of our opponents. St. Mary's of Glens Falls would be made up of tough Irish Catholics. We could expect the Ft. Edward team to consist of rough Italians. The Whitehall players would be the rugged sons of marble quarry workers. Granville would field sinewy Polish linemen and fullbacks with names made up mainly of consonants. Glens Falls, of course, would send out a host of swaggering "city" kids.

Nevertheless, we finished the season with three victories and two ties, knotted with Granville for the conference championship. We won the big War Bond benefit play-off game that followed, 7-0. It was no scoring spree, but it was a victory. A week later, I opened the *Post-Star* sports page and was surprised to find I was one of four Hudson Falls players named to the All-Conference team. Eleanor and I celebrated that night with malted milk shakes at Baker's Drug Store.

Shortly after that some friends and I were in Glens Falls when the bus from Albany arrived. Two young men in leather Army Air Force jackets got out, picked up their green B-4 bags, and stood

The author and Eleanor Baker in 1943, before he entered the Air Force

waiting for the trip to Hudson Falls. We knew them; they had graduated from high school the previous June, and were home on leave after finishing gunnery school training. They were dashing in uniforms bearing colorful shoulder patches, silver gunner's wings, and fresh corporal's stripes.

The dramatic return of those men, as well as my early interest in airplanes, made me quite receptive when "Muff" Nassivera, our football quarterback, suggested that we enlist in the Air Force rather than wait to be drafted into the Army. We would become pilots, of course; every boy worth his salt wanted to be one. I quickly agreed. The infantry held little appeal.

I told my father that I intended to join the Air Force. "Do what you think best," he said. There were few other choices. I don't remember telling Chuck my plans. I assumed that he would go into the Army.

Booklets that contained tips on ways to pass military tests were available in the 1940s. I bought one and studied it carefully. There were drawings of blocks stacked in uneven rows in a corner, and of interlocking gears. One had to calculate how many blocks were in the pile and the direction in which the last gear would be turned. It was rather basic stuff, but I did not want to take a chance at being rejected.

I rode the bus to Albany for the first time. The Air Force recruiting station was located in a downtown office building. After taking the written exam, I was interviewed by a young lieutenant.

"What's the equation for the area of a circle?" he asked.

"Pi R squared."

"Have you ever driven a motorcycle?"

I knew what he was looking for — an adventurous future fighter pilot. "No, but I loved open-field running in football." That should impress him, I thought.

"What's an isosceles triangle?" I was stumped. I knew it well, but for some reason it just wouldn't come. He nodded and said nothing. On the bus on the way home, I remembered that it was a triangle with two equal sides — of course. I went home feeling disappointed.

It made little difference. I was accepted, and told to wait for further orders after my physical examination and high school graduation. The examination took place in the National Guard Armory in Albany, a grim, old stone fortress of a building. Several of us boarded a bus to go down for the tests. The group included a man who was both our high school track coach and commercial studies teacher. He was married and nearly beyond draft age. We entered the armory, stripped down to our undershorts, and spent the day being probed, weighed and measured.

At the end of the day I walked down a long stairway. A Marine officer was at the bottom, looking over the men as they descended. He caught my eye.

"Are you sure you don't want to be a Marine?"

"I'm sure," I answered. I was patriotic, but not to that degree. I have since wondered what would have happened had I accepted that invitation, for the bloody amphibious landings at Saipan, Iwo Jima and Okinawa still lay ahead.

When we gathered for the trip home, the teacher was beaming.

"How did it go, coach?"

"I didn't pass," he said. "Flat feet." Despite the ignominy of 4-F status, he was happy to have it.

Basketball season followed, as did long walks with "Bake" (for

Baker) on crystal-clear winter nights. We held mittened hands and stole frosty kisses as we crunched over the snow. A week after my high school graduation my first draft notice arrived. It was a mimeographed form letter from a major in the headquarters of the Second Service Command on Governor's Island, with only my name and date filled in. It sent a chill through me.

"Private Andrew M. Doty

1. This is to advise you that you are being called upon to active duty on or about 31 January 1944.

2. Orders will be sent to you within the next few days."

Soon after that, my induction notice arrived. "Greetings," it began. "You have been chosen by a board made up of your friends and neighbors to serve in the armed forces of the United States of America for the duration of the war. You will report to the Induction Center at Ft. Dix, N.J. on January 31, 1944." It was signed by the elderly chairman of our local draft board in behalf of his elderly fellow board members.

Bake and I walked to her father's drug store that night and took our places in a rear booth. I showed her the two letters.

"They don't waste any words, do they?" she said.

"Not at all. They didn't even say 'please' report."

"I'm glad that you have a few weeks left."

Other than that, she said little. We were still in the formal stage of our relationship, and had not spoken of love. We did not even admit how greatly we would miss each other. My time simply had come.

"I have a feeling this will take about two years," I said as we walked slowly back down Mechanic Street.

"Oh," she said. "That long?"

Chapter Three
Into Uniform

The Waite Hose Company hall on Main Street was the scene of frequent farewell parties in those times. One was held for Chuck and me the week before we were to enter the military. We received some gifts and said goodbye to our friends. Chuck left the week before I did, bound for Camp Upton on Long Island. As his train pulled out of the D & H station he pretended to wipe tears from his eye, hiding his sorrow with humor.

The night before I was to leave I visited Bake at her house. We had known each other only a short time, but I cared for her and was sorry to say good-bye. I went home early and sadly — early because I should spend most of the time with my parents and sadly because of the long separation and uncertainty that lay ahead.

"Write to me," she called out as I walked off her porch.

"I will," I said. "It should be interesting."

My mother and father watched silently as I packed my new toilet kit and stationery into a bag, along with a small Bible that my sister Ruth had sent me. What were my parents thinking? How it must have torn them to see their twin sons leave within a week of each other, but they did not say a word. It was our turn, and there could be no complaint. Thirty years later I fought off tears as my oldest daughter left home safely to attend college only one state away. How did our parents keep from breaking down as Chuck and I went off to war? Perhaps they did after we were gone.

The last day of January was bitterly cold. Mom, Dad and I silently ate breakfast before Ken Howe arrived in the early morning darkness to drive me to Glens Falls to catch the bus to Albany. I said goodbye to them as quickly as I could. As Ken and I sat in his car waiting for the bus, a boy rode up on his bicycle. He was Gerry Ellsworth, a classmate who lived two miles outside of the city. He had ridden in to see me off, despite the frigid weather. I was touched by his thoughtfulness.

The New York Central railroad station in Albany was an exciting place in those days. It had marble floors, hardwood benches, and towering ceilings. There was a USO area on a balcony where uniformed women volunteers passed out coffee to the servicemen. The station teemed with soldiers, sailors and marines and echoed with their clamor and train announcements. It was the first time I had been there. I felt that I was entering the serious world of adults.

Alone on the train to New York, I saw my reflection in the window and wondered what would become of that young man. I wore the gray and white Hart, Schaefner and Marx herringbone suit I had proudly bought with my summer earnings, a tan shirt, and a wine tie. I was sad and apprehensive and excited. How long would I be gone? What lay ahead?

The train sped down the banks of the Hudson River, past the old Dutch towns and cities, and into New York. We dove underground with a roar and emerged in cavernous Grand Central Station. The huge, vaulted area was crowded with hundreds of servicemen and women of all kinds and ranks. The Albany station that had impressed me so much would be swallowed up in this one.

While waiting to transfer to Penn Station and start the trip to Trenton, where I would catch a bus to Ft. Dix, I ventured out onto the busy sidewalk. I made it safely to a Nedicks orange juice stand, a few hundred feet away. I dared go no further for fear of getting lost. As I stood at the stand with my drink, a man came in and called out to the clerk. "Gimme a vanalla milk shake."

Without a word, the clerk dropped a glass heavily on the counter in front of the customer. He scooped ice cream into a metal container, splashed in some milk, and jammed the can into a mixer. When it was done, he removed the container and poured the shake into the glass. The customer jabbed his finger at the glass. "All of it! All of it!" he demanded. The clerk glared, shook the few remaining drops into the glass, then sent the container clattering into the sink.

I was amazed. Is that the way they treat people around here? It was. At Ft. Dix, the huge, multi-floor concrete barracks contained several loud, vulgar men, seemingly all from Brooklyn or New Jersey. I consoled myself with the fact that they were Army recruits, not Air Force. Then I remembered that Chuck had gone into the infantry.

After arriving at Ft. Dix I took off my new suit, packed it in a box, and mailed it home. I traded it for more clothing than I had owned in my entire lifetime: duffel bags filled with khaki shirts, trousers, socks, and underwear; a heavy overcoat, gloves, a knit cap, and GI shoes. We shuffled past warehouse bins filled with metal mess kits, ponchos, and light helmet liners, tossing the items into our bags as we moved along. I also gained a new identity — serial number 42120238, embossed on metal "dog tags" to hang around my neck.

A piercing bugle call on the barracks PA system shocked us awake early every morning that week. Knit caps pulled down over our ears, overcoats hanging to our ankles, we stumbled onto the dark, frigid company street. We fell into formation, slapping our arms, stamping our feet, our breath billowing out in front of us.

Then came the first of many manglings of a name that goes far back into English history. But the hard-bitten master sergeant was not aware of that. "Dotty?" the sergeant called. "Duty?" "Here!" I answered, before any more damage could be done. It was hard to understand how he - and his successors at later roll calls - could butcher a name so badly.

The indignities of military life have been well chronicled: hair shorn almost to the scalp, long rows of toilets with no partitions between them, "short arm" inspections by doctors at our bunks at unannounced times, and demands of unquestioning obedience. Our individual identities were being stripped away. We received a battery of immunization shots, learned to count off and march in formation, and attended an irrelevant lecture on the dangers of venereal disease.

Our orientation completed, we boarded a troop train bound for basic training at Greensboro, North Carolina. As the miles clicked beneath the car, I speculated on how long it would be before the distance was retraced. We disembarked at the camp. Spread out on the red, sloping hills were row upon row of low-lying barracks. Squads of men marched along the streets, counting off cadence and chanting songs. As we formed up and moved off, the others shouted "You'll be so-o-o-o-r-r-y!" and "Here come more gunners." The latter was a shock; we thought we were destined for preflight training. The shouts were another touch of reality. Later on, we took pleasure in repeating them to the new batches of recruits we saw arriving.

The smell of burning soft coal will remind me forever of our six weeks at Greensboro. It came from the two iron stoves in each building, and clung in the wet air as we marched from class to class in our ponchos and helmet liners. We would sit on the hard floor of an empty barracks to hear lessons about poison gases, camouflage techniques, and carbine nomenclature.

Our drill sergeant was a ruddy-faced southerner who wore sharply creased trousers and shirts, and highly polished shoes. His cap was set at a precise military angle, and he insisted that ours be positioned exactly the same way. He stood straight and tall. He briskly herded us about, shouting commands and calling out the cadence:

"Hup, two, three, four
Hup, two, three, four
Hup, two, three, four.
You had a good job and you left;
You had a good job and you left;
Your left, your left, you had a good job and you left.
Your left, your left,
You had a good job and you left — your right,
You had a good job and you left — your right.
You had a good job and you left."

The beat was strong and irresistible. So were the marching songs, which made long hikes about the base almost pleasant. We had become a unit, and actually enjoyed it at times.

We struck up a steady rhythm as we swung along, singing "I've Been Working on the Railroad," "Into the Air, Army Air Corps," and "Around Her Neck, She Wore a Yellow Ribbon" (for her airman who was "far, far away.") The second verse was quickly corrupted to "around the block, she wheels a baby carriage." Singing, marching, chanting, joking and griping made our lives much more tolerable.

The sergeant was an Army career man who shaped batches of clumsy civilians into fairly respectable soldiers. He taught us to run through the manual of arms smartly with our carbines, to salute properly, and to don a gas mask in minutes. When we failed to measure up, he chewed us out unmercifully.

"What a piss-poor excuse for soldiers y'all are," he told us early one morning for some good reason. "Y'all don't fall out on time, ya don't get the drill raht, ya don't salute raht, ya don't do nothin' raht. We're gonna lose this goddamn war sure as hell if it's up to the likes a y'all."

"That's a double negative, Sarge," someone offered.

"What? What'n hell do you mean?"

"That we don't do nothing right — that means we do something right."

"You do like hell. This is the saddest lookin' bunch that's ever come through here. I swear to hell we're gettin' to the bottom of the goddamn barrel. The krauts must be lickin' their chops to get at the likes a you sad bastards."

A member of our squad was standing in the darkness in the back row. With his lips pursed and unmoving, he muttered: "Blow it out your ass."

"What? WHAT? Who said that? Who said that?" the sergeant demanded, glaring into the formation. He paced in front of us, staring at each man.

"Somebody's buckin' for a year a KP, and he's gonna get it. Who's the smartass? Who's the smartass?" There was no answer.

"All right, you guys — twenty-five push-ups, ev'ry goddamn one of ya, raht nahw."

We dropped to the ground to do as he said, but we were smiling among ourselves. Even a touch of revenge felt good.

A Greensboro boy would come into the barracks at night to sell newspapers. He was often met by a chorus of cries.

"Here comes another Rebel," someone called out. "Nail everything down."

"Grab your wallets, men."

"Don't let him outa sight."

The boy strode down the long aisle between the double bunks, looking straight ahead. "Fuck-in' Yan-kees," he said, drawing out the words with a marvelous drawl.

Our turn came for KP - Kitchen Police. Innocent as a babe, I showed up at the mess hall on my assigned morning. The older

Eleanor Baker, the author's high school sweetheart and wartime correspondent.

hands on the base disappeared magically into jobs that lasted only through each meal, ladling out oatmeal or scrambled eggs. I ended up at a huge sink, washing pots and pans by hand. The sun rose on the far side of the building as I stood there, and it set behind me as I scoured. I was at the sink most of the day. Just when I thought those of us who remained were finished, an officer came into the kitchen, tested the silverware with a glove, and ruled that it was so greasy that it had to be washed again with vinegar.

Mail call was the high point of each day. We went down to the mail room and waited to hear our names, or renditions of them, called out. "Yo," we shouted, and picked up our letters. There often was one from Bake, for we had begun to write frequently. I saved her letter for last and looked for some sign that she cared for me. She generally signed them "Love." Later, it was "All my love" or "Much love." "SWAK" — Sealed With a Kiss — began to appear on the back of the envelopes, along with a lipstick imprint. I was pleased by that show of affection. After a while, she sent me a photo of herself, auburn hair falling to her shoulders. I kept it in my box of writing materials and studied it often.

Pay day saw long lines of airmen waiting in front of a table. An officer sat with a log book containing our names and serial numbers. As we stood there, a soldier glanced at the sky.

"Looks like it might cloud up and rain," he said.

A big, black sergeant stood behind me. "I don't care if it cloud up and *shits,*" he said, " Ah'm gonna stay here and get my money."

That night men gathered in a corner of the barracks to shoot dice. Some walked away with fistfuls of bills. Others had lost all, or most, of their monthly earnings, and soon were borrowing from their friends. I did not understand how they could be so foolish.

We set out one day on a twelve-mile hike to a rifle range, carrying carbines, packs and gas masks. It was a long, hot trip. As we neared the range, tired and sweaty, a jeep roared past, releasing a cloud of tear gas. Eyes burning, we fumbled for our gas masks and swore vigorously at the disappearing vehicle. It was a good lesson, but we failed to appreciate it.

At the range we lived in tents, ate from mess kits, and spent the days firing rifles and pistols at targets. We were eighteen years old. Stretched out in our cots at night, we could hear far-off train whistles and were homesick.

Chapter Four
Gunnery School

Back at the main camp, we took tests to find out if we could enter pre-flight training. The end of the war in Europe was in sight, so fewer cadets were being chosen for the lengthy program. Only one man from our group was selected. I was so ashamed that for days I could not bring myself to write home that I would be going into gunnery school instead of pre-flight classes.

We packed our gear, shouldered it all, and marched off to the railroad tracks and a waiting train. Our sergeant shook our hands and wished us well.

"Y'all are going to do okay," he said. "You shaped up good."

We boarded a "cattle car" troop train that contained rows of bunk beds. I liked the arrangement; instead of Pullman berths that forced two men to share a wide lower bunk, there were rows of individual bunks on floor-to-ceiling steel legs. In between the bunks were wide aisles. We could move about freely in the open areas, and nap or read on our bunks during the day. No serviceman will ever forget the smell of the smoke that wafted back from the engine, or the grit that sifted through cracks and covered everything.

Standing patiently in the long chow lines with our mess kits, we were jostled by the movement of the cars. Looking out the windows, we were introduced to the poverty of the rural South. As I watched the shacks and small towns of Georgia, Alabama, Mississippi and Louisiana slide by, I realized how fortunate I had been to grow up in our river valley village. The railroad crossing arms would be down as the train sped along the drab main streets, bells ringing as we shot past, the men waving and shouting at the girls as the girls waved back. Sometimes the train would halt in the middle of a town; the most adventuresome men would race to a nearby store and run back with all the beer they could carry before the train moved on.

We were on our way to the air base at Harlingen, Texas. The school was near the Gulf Coast, just above Mexico. We arrived at night, picked up our bedding, and retired. I awoke in the morning to find myself in a world unlike any I had ever seen. Suddenly it was summer: there were palm trees, soft warm breezes, and suntan uniforms. High in the cloudless skies, four-engine bombers droned continually on their training flights.

Our six weeks of gunnery school was a fascinating experience. There was no KP or other drudgery; we were a privileged class being readied for war. It was a grand adventure, still unrelated to the deadly aerial battles then taking place over Europe. Our instructors told us about the piercing cold in a bomber at high altitude, about the damage that anti-aircraft fire can inflict, and about the way bullets were deflected by the shielding on the front of an attacking Focke Wulf fighter, but it did not really sink in. Much of that was due to the matter-of-fact way in which the information was presented, without reference to death, wounds, or downed crews. I had a distinct feeling that one of our instructors in particular, a staff sergeant who had flown twenty-five missions with the Eighth Air Force over Germany and looked older than his years, was sparing us the worst details. He held himself apart, and I sensed that he felt sorry for us.

One day at a range where we learned to fire machine guns, I asked an older ground attendant if he had ever flown. "Are you crazy? he answered. "I've seen them wash too many of you guys out of a crash with a hose."

It was a sobering statement, but we laughed when I repeated it that night in the barracks. We were seated in an auditorium another time when an officer casually told us that a third of the men in the room would be killed, wounded or taken prisoner. I felt sorry for the others, for surely nothing could happen to me. Youth is optimistic, feels indestructible, and sees life as infinite. Thus young people ride bicycles blindly around corners, drive cars too fast, and fight wars.

I wondered how they would teach me to kill another man. I hated fist fights, never hunted animals, and always tried to be kind to others. What would they do to change my nature? The answer is easy: they simply give you the training, the equipment, some indoctrination, and the opportunity. You can either shoot back, or regret it. And of course you could not let your buddies down, or be seen as cowardly.

Whatever was needed, we worked into gradually. There were slide shows of German, Japanese, American and British aircraft. We called out the names of the Zeros, Spitfires, ME 109's, Lightnings, Nicks, P-47s, P-51s and Focke Wulfs as they flashed by. As a model builder and an airplane freak for so many years, I found it all very familiar.

Then came a turn with guns that fired a stream of BB pellets at a model airplane that moved on a track across a painted canvas sky. What adventurous boy could resist that game? It was good, clean, harmless fun. We peppered the model as it emerged from behind a "cloud" and sped across an open expanse.

Later we went out to a skeet range, where we fired shotguns at circular clay pigeons as they were catapulted in front of us. Leading the black saucers by a radius or two, we shattered them by the hour. There must be a stratum of broken birds several feet thick at that site today.

We graduated from the stationary skeet range to the back of an open truck that circled an oval track. Catapult stations were located at various points along the route. We stood in the back of the vehicle and took turns firing our shotguns at the skimming targets as we drove along, compensating for both the movement of the truck and the trajectory of the birds.

One morning we were marched to a large classroom building. Inside was an area that contained several metal-topped tables. Mounted on a pedestal at one table was a large, black, lethal-looking machine gun. An instructor stood in front of us, his arm resting on the gun.

"Men, this here is a 50-caliber, Browning M2 machine gun. It is a belt-fed, recoil-operated, air-cooled weapon. It can fire twelve to fourteen rounds a second, maximum, but that would burn out the gun barrel fast if you kept it up for long. So don't ever do it. Instead, we rapid-fire forty rounds a minute, in bursts of six to nine rounds, at five to ten-second intervals to save the barrel.

"Before you're done, you're gonna learn this baby inside-out and backwards. If you don't, it could be your ass, and I don't mean maybe. So listen careful."

We did just that in the weeks that followed. The 50-caliber was a brute of a weapon, heavy, accurate, and rapid-firing. It weighed eighty pounds, and could shoot half-inch diameter bullets more than four miles with a muzzle velocity of 2,900 feet a second. Its most effective range was up to 600 yards.

Day after day, we took the gun apart, learning the name and function of every piece. I removed the rear buffer plate, examined the buffer discs, released the driving spring rod, and withdrew the shiny steel bolt assembly. I could not help but admire the smooth, beautifully-machined unit that pulled the rounds steadily into the gun, slammed them into the breech, fired, recoiled, ejected the clips and cartridges, then repeated the process. We were shown how to keep the gun oiled and in good repair, and how to clear malfunctions. The day finally came when I could put on a blindfold, dismantle the weapon, spread the parts out on the table, then put them all back together. I smiled with satisfaction after the job was completed.

A machine gun firing range was located in the sand dunes near the Gulf Coast. Rows of 50s were mounted on steel pedestals, facing targets half a mile away. Holding a bucking gun by its two handles, I sent a torrent of bullets into a target area, creating geysers of sand and dust. The noise hammered my ears and the brass cases spewed into the air as long belts of ammunition were devoured. I did not let myself think about a similar stream of enemy slugs that someday could come flying back in my direction.

The next step was a visit to a large hangar at Harlingen that contained heavy wooden platforms. Mounted on them were the electrically-driven nose, ball and tail turrets that were found in B-24 Liberator bombers. Each turret contained two fifty-caliber machine guns. We learned how to operate each of the turrets, swinging the units from side to side, and the guns up and down. The nose and tail turrets were like tiny greenhouses perched out on the edge of nowhere. I felt highly vulnerable sitting in them, surrounded only by thin, clear plastic.

The Sperry ball turret hung below the fuselage of both the B-24 and the B-17 Flying Fortress to protect the underbelly of the bombers. The turret was a metal and Plexiglas "goldfish bowl" about three feet in diameter. It called for smaller men who could curl up inside for long periods of time. The B-24 ball had to be raised from its position beneath the plane so that the gunner could enter. The turret then was lowered into place. We prac-

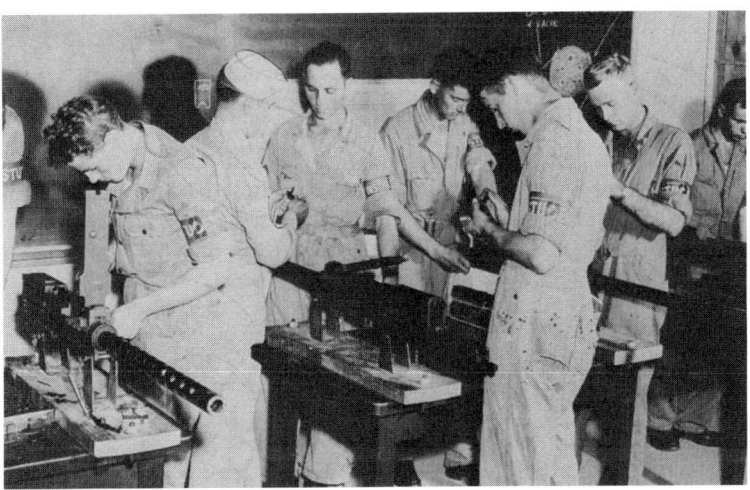

Gunnery school students learning the nomenclature of the Browning 50-caliber machine gun. At the end of their training, they could take the gun apart and reassemble it while blindfolded. Courtesy Air Force Gunners Association

A gunnery student receives instruction on the operation of a turret used to defend bombers against attacking enemy fighter planes. U.S. Air Museum photo

ticed the routine on the platform. The ball would be brought up, secured, and the hatch opened. I would climb in, the hatch would be closed overhead, and the ball would be eased downward. Today, the memory of the practice gives me claustrophobic shivers; at that time, it was simply another command to be obeyed.

In still another classroom an instructor described the famous Air Force clock system for reporting the positions of attacking aircraft. "Twelve o'clock" was directly ahead of the bomber, "three o'clock" was off the right wing tip, "six o'clock" behind the tail, and so on. Accordingly, a fighter closing in at "seven o'clock low" was to the lower right of the tail gunner, and one at "twelve o'clock high" was approaching the pilots from above.

The instructor held up a model of a German Me 109 fighter. "Suppose I'm a German sittin' out here like this at three o' clock, checkin' you out and gettin' ready to come in," he said. He positioned the model as if it were flying parallel to the front row of our class, the nose pointing to our left.

"Here's what to look for. You watch his inner wing tip like a hawk. If the guy is really serious, the wing will tilt up, and he'll come sweeping in and drop back toward the tail of your plane, like this." He tipped the wing up and let the plane fall off to our right, the nose pointed steadily at us.

"That's called a pursuit curve. It holds the fighter right on target every inch of the way. If the guy is a little chicken — sometimes they are — he'll dip the inner wing down and cut around behind you, like this." He showed us how the fighter would bank sharply down and away to its left.

"That's a fly-through. It means that his fire will be scattered and much less accurate, like a hose sweepin' across a lawn instead of being pointed straight at you all the time. You'll like that."

"And for God's sake, don't waste your ammunition on a fighter flying alongside you way out here, doing no harm. Hold your fire until he starts coming in. You're going to need every round you've got."

With those heartening words, we were ready to take to the air.

Chapter Five
Into the Air

Several AT-6 training planes awaited us on the flight line at Harlingen one morning. They were low-wing, single-engine aircraft with an open cockpit in the rear. A thirty-caliber machine gun — the "little" brother of the fifty — was mounted behind the cockpit. We were handed leather helmets, goggles, parachute harnesses and parachutes, and told how to use them. A sergeant gathered us around a trainer. He told us we would be flown out to the Gulf, where we would fire at targets as we flew low over the water.

"Two things," he said, holding up his fingers. "One, don't shoot the tail off the airplane. If you do, somebody's going to be mad as hell, including the pilot. Second, remember to space your bursts. If you don't, you'll burn out the barrel, then I'll be mad."

Several of my companions flew first. Some returned swallowing hard, or with less color in their faces. When my turn came, I put on my equipment and climbed into the rear seat for my first airplane ride. The bored pilot sped out to the runway, paused as briefly as a bird on a bush, then roared into the air. Looking down at the countryside, I was exhilarated. The houses, barns and cars were small toys far below. We continued toward the Gulf. Suddenly the plane banked, dropped, and swooped across the shallow water. I fired at the floating targets, taking care to do as I had been told. The bullets tore into the water, coming near a Mexican fishing boat that had strayed into the area to pick up stunned fish. A man dove overboard, not knowing that I had no intention of hitting the boat.

An aerial gunner's first flight in an AT-6 training plane. *Courtesy USAL/NASM*

We repeated the run, then returned to the base. In retrospect, the main objective of the flight may have been to see if we were fit to fly. If we managed to hit the water, did not get sick, missed the tail and spared the gun barrel, we passed.

We began flying in different kinds of bombers as the pilots practiced piloting, the navigators navigating, the bombardiers bombing, and the gunners, gunning. We donned fleece-lined helmets, jackets, pants, gloves and boots and clambered into an old B-24 Liberator bomber. It roared down the runway, lifted from the ground and slowly climbed upward. After a time, we put on our oxygen masks and plugged the long hoses into the ship's system. Standing beside an open waist window some 25,000 feet in the sky, I marveled at the clarity of the air, the brilliance of the sunshine, and the vapor trails that formed long streamers behind our plane. Flight at those altitudes in those days was an adventure requiring heavy clothing and oxygen masks. Today it is commonplace to fly comfortably six miles above the earth in pressurized cabins.

High above Texas one April afternoon, a B-24 ball turret was raised, and the hatch opened.

"Your turn," our instructor said to me. "In you go."

I settled myself into the compartment and connected my oxygen tube and intercom line. The hatch was closed and latched above me. The twin-fifties and I were pointed straight down at the ground, thousands of feet below. The turret was slowly lowered into the sparkling air. Using upright hand levers that pivoted in all directions, I leveled the turret and rotated it so that I could look all about. Overhead was the fat underside of our bomber and its big, oval twin rudders; around me was the vast sky. A camera was mounted in the turret to record simulated attacks by friendly fighters. One appeared from below — an old Bell P-39 Airacobra, coming straight on. I fixed him in my gun sight, pushed the firing buttons on top of the levers with my thumbs, and "shot" him with my camera. It was an exciting moment.

Between flights we went to classes, learned survival techniques, and studied our manuals. I remember sitting in the lighted stairway of our barracks one night, reading a lesson after the rest of the building had been darkened. To "wash out" of gunnery school would have been a terrible disgrace, far worse than missing out on pre-flight training. If I failed I could be sent to the Air Transport Command, where I would spend the war safely loading freight into cargo planes instead of flying missions over enemy territory. That was a fate to be avoided. The boy who never hunted animals now was willing to shoot at other men — or would be chagrined not to be shooting at them. I had not hardened or developed a killer instinct; I was simply responding to the pressures of the time.

I did not feel fear while suspended below the bomber, nor did I question the assignment. I should have; the turret was top-heavy, and could swing violently if not locked into place inside the airplane as I was sliding in or out. And if the ship's electrical system were knocked out, the ball turret could not be retracted. Worst of all, there was no room in the ball for a parachute. One was totally dependent upon the crewmen above to raise the turret, secure it, and help one get out to put on a 'chute.

It occurred to me that if my bomber was aflame and spinning to earth, the crewmen above might well decide to save themselves rather than lose time retrieving me. How many ball turret gunners plunged to their deaths in World War II in the same fetal position in which they had begun their lives? Their casualty rate was high. Despite the problems, I continued on, and was destined for duty beneath a bomber when our training period came to an end. I had inherited my parents' stoicism, or their optimism, or both.

Our daily calisthenics exercises saw acres of lean, tanned men, wearing white shorts and black sneakers, swinging arms high and legs wide in chanted unison. Watching them, I speculated on the thousands of other young men at other bases around the world who at that same moment were preparing in the same way to do battle against their enemies.

"Look!" someone called out as we were returning from our mess hall after dinner one evening. He pointed to a B-24 with a smoking engine that was swinging low over the base, racing toward the landing strip. We stopped to watch the bomber bank sharply downward and drop from sight beyond the barracks. Soon a pillar of black smoke rose high in the sky. As I lay in my bed that night I imagined myself in the place of that crew in its terrifying plunge to earth. Later we learned that the bomber had leveled out to land and burn, and that everyone had escaped unhurt.

Late in our stay at Harlingen, we were given a treat: a one-day pass to visit Matamoras, Mexico, just across the Rio Grande from nearby Brownsville. First we heard a lecture by a flight surgeon.

"Gentlemen," he said. "You are about to visit another country, where some real temptations will be laid in front of you, if I may say so. I know some of you are so horny you can hardly stand it, but I would encourage you to be very, very careful. There is a lot of disease over there so I strongly advise you to keep it in your pants. If you don't, by all means take along some protection. Remember, you want to go back home to your wives and girl friends in the same good health you left them." His comments made good sense to me.

A bus took us to Brownsville, where we looked across a muddy little trickle of water. The Rio Grande hardly lived up to its name, but I was excited to see the famous international boundary.

The flight surgeon's words, and the location of a prophylactics station at the U.S. end of the bridge over the river, should have told us something. Older GIs were streaming from the station and into Matamoras. Three of us followed them into town, only to find ourselves in a dusty, uninteresting square with stunted trees. We took seats at an outdoor cafe to drink Mexican beer. A soldier approached.

"I hear there's a great night club in this town," he said, "but you can only get there by taxi. You guys wanta chip in on the fare?"

Sure, we said, and off we went. The narrow streets became ever shabbier as the old taxi edged through them. Young girls and women were lounging in the windows and doorways of the buildings. We got out of the car to walk toward the "club." As we did, a small boy ran beside us and pulled at our sleeves.

"Fuckee my sister, she virgin," he said, pointing toward a house. He made the same offer to some soldiers behind us. We pressed on and entered the building. It took time for our eyes to become accustomed to the gloom. Then we saw young women in scanty outfits moving toward us. They reached out to our arms and stroked our bodies. "Buy me drink?" they asked. "Buy me drink?"

We shook our heads and took seats at a table, where we ordered beer and watched the scene. The room was filled with soldiers who were dancing with women or sat them on their laps, openly fondling them. A large older woman sat at an ancient cash register, holding a baby. The GIs would go to her, pay a few dollars, and disappear through a doorway with their girls. The woman would ring up the sale with a clang. We finished our beers and left, again running the sad gauntlet of little boys hustling business for their sisters.

Back at Harlingen, we took a battery of tests, received our silver wings and corporal's stripes, and were ready for assignment to a combat squadron. We were rolling out of gunnery schools across the south and southwest every week by the hundreds, ready to join the shiny new bombers that were steadily flowing off their own production lines.

We hoped to go home on leave after gunnery school, but that was not to be; we packed our gear and boarded another troop train, this one headed north across Texas and into Colorado. I sat by a window and watched the snow-capped peaks of the Rockies shining to our left as we traveled the length of the state.

A handsome young airman with a soft southern accent took the seat beside me. His car had been joined to our troop train during one of the innumerable long stops during the night. We introduced ourselves and shook hands.

"Where are you from?" he asked.

"New York state. Hudson Falls. It's a town fifty-two miles above Albany on the Vermont border. Right on the Hudson River."

"Never heard of it," he said. "How big is it?"

"Seven thousand people. But it's a pretty place. Where are you from?"

"College Park, Georgia. Outside of Atlanta. Ah believe it's one of the garden spots of the world."

The word "Atlanta" rolled off his tongue in a soft way that is foreign to northerners.

"How long you been in?" he asked.

"Since February first. I was inducted at Ft. Dix, then took basic at Greensboro. It rained most of the time. How about you?

"Last Fall. I went to Greensboro, too. Then I went to the aircraft mechanics school at Keesler Field in Mississippi for a while. But I got tired of that stuff so's me an another guy volunteered to go to gunnery school."

The author at the age of eighteen, proudly wearing his new aerial gunner's wings at Harlingen, Texas in 1944.

With fellow gunner Jim Dudley of College Park, Georgia.

"What school?

"Laredo. That's where we're coming from now. Not much goin' on there, I can tell you that."

"How many in your family?" he asked after a time.

"Seven of us. I've got four sisters and two brothers. One brother is my twin. He's in the infantry at Camp Blanding in Florida. My older brother is on a tank assembly line back home. My sisters are all working."

"What's your father do?

"He's a papermaker at the mill in Hudson Falls. He works hard."

"What's your twin like?"

"He's different. We're fraternal twins. He's more like my father. I'm more like my mother.

"That must mean you don't work hard."

"You got me there. How many in your family?"

"I'm the only one. You're lucky to have all those brothers and sisters."

"What position did you train for at Laredo?" I asked.

"Nose, tail, waist - everything but the ball turret. I couldn't fit in one, and wouldn't get in even if I could. A guy's gotta be out of his mind to do that. Where have you been?"

"Harlingen. Down by the Gulf."

"What position?"

"The ball turret. "

"Oh." There was a long pause as we looked out at the distant mountains.

"Where do you suppose we're headed?" he asked.

"Beats me. Could be Alaska for all I know. They didn't ask where I wanted to go."

"Ain't that the truth," he replied.

I was immediately intrigued by his drawl, and by his use of the phrase "Ah believe." "Ah believe that's the Continental Divide over yonder," he said. "Ah believe we're coming into Denver just now." My companion's name was Jim Dudley. We were destined to spend some of the most dramatic moments of our lives together in the coming months.

We were en route to the air base at Fairmont, Nebraska, where we would receive more intensive training. Once we had settled in at Fairmont, we were given our two-week home leaves. Jim started back to the garden spot of the world while and I boarded a train bound for Chicago, Buffalo, Albany and home.

My train ride was a happy one. While waiting in Chicago to transfer to the New York Central train, I walked outside the station to look down on the city's canals and bridges and up at the tall buildings. I am really seeing the world, I thought.

The train rolled across Illinois, Ohio and New York. The fields and hills of the East were green. I had forgotten the full crowns of the elms and maples and the canopies that overhung the quiet villages along our route. Later, standing in the open area between the cars of the Delaware and Hudson Railroad on the way from Albany to Ft. Edward, I drank in the beautiful Hudson Valley countryside. Despite its nickname, the "Delay and Halt" railroad soon delivered me to the Ft. Edward station on a fine summer day. I was tanned and trim, a bit more seasoned than the boy who had left home three months earlier, and was filled with the delicious anticipation of seeing my family and Bake again.

After Chuck and I had gone into service, Mom and Dad had moved into the home of my cousin Ruth, whose husband had become the P-47 mechanic. I took the bus from Ft. Edward to Hudson Falls and carried my bags out Maple Street, across the old Barge Canal, and onto Coombs Avenue on the edge of town. Dad and Ruth were at work, and Mom greeted me at the door.

"Oh, Andrew, you're back," she said, and hugged me. "How long will you be home?"

"Two weeks."

"Chuck is coming home later this month," she said. "Maybe they'll let you stay on to see him."

"I doubt that, but I'll try." The next day I walked up to Moriarty's to send a telegram to the base, asking for a one-week extension of my furlough. A duty officer lost no time in replying "Request denied," his telegram read. "Return to Fairmont as scheduled."

I still have in my files the note that I left for Chuck just before I returned to Nebraska at the end of my leave.

"Hiya Chuck," it reads. "Home again. Hope you read this soon. The war looks damn good today. It'll be over in '45, I think. And then — back to mufti by nineteen-fufty. See you, Andy."

The two weeks melted away. I visited relatives and friends by day, and met Bake after her summer job in a Sand Hill Iron and Brass office. She wore light sleeveless summer dresses with a scooped neck, and had slender, tanned arms and legs. We would stroll up to the village park in the evening or walk around the shaded side streets. Later we would find our way back to the glider on her front porch.

Harry Baker's "Square Deal" Drug Store was open six and one-half days a week. He worked late every night; a pharmacist always had to be on duty, and he was the only one. Before he locked up the store he would call to find out what kind of ice cream his wife wanted him to bring home.

Mrs. Baker would come to the screen door to ask if we wanted any. Of course we did; that was one the fringe benefits of being a druggist's daughter, or of dating one, and cholesterol had yet to be invented. Soon Harry would arrive on his ancient bike, carrying a package and puffing slightly from his asthma. He was a short man, with a round tummy and a tuft of white hair on his bald head. He had penetrating blue eyes and a short upturned nose. He was direct and totally honest. He was one of the most respected men in town. Often his white pharmacist's jacket would be smudged with chocolate or butterscotch from helping out during busy times at the ice cream fountain.

Charlotte Baker was a strong, good-looking woman who could remove, wash, iron and return every curtain in her big brick house in a single spring cleaning day — and prepare three full meals in between. She was a Royal Matron in the Order of the Amaranth. She also watched over her daughter with the instincts of an Iranian chaperone. After the ice cream was dished out, we would take our places on the porch. Bake and I claimed the glider as her parents sat in their green chairs.

"What did you do today, Andy ?" Mrs. Baker would ask.

"Not much. I went down to see Agnes and Leah for a while. There's nobody around. I spent some time up in the park with some of the younger guys."

"What do you hear from your friend Bob Burns?"

"I got a letter just before I left. Bob's in Navy boot camp over at Sampson. He says they've taught him how to tie a knot in each leg of a pair of pants in an emergency and jump into the water in a way that fills the legs fill up with air to form a kind of life preserver."

"I wonder how long he could stay afloat with that arrangement," Mr. Baker said.

"I don't know. I'd sure hate to try it."

"Please don't," Bake said.

After we had finished our sundaes and milk shakes, we would do the dishes. Then it was time for her parents to retire. I would not leave before they went to bed.

We were still innocent. We sat on the porch glider, slowly swinging, Bake's legs tucked up under her as I held her in my arms on the warm summer nights. She had touched the very lightest of colognes to her skin. Large elm branches cast shadows on the porch, and a bit of light filtered through from the street lamps. Crickets sounded all about us.

Time drifted by, neither of us willing to end the evening. We whispered so that we would not disturb her mother and father, who were sleeping in a downstairs bedroom. Harry Baker may have been slumbering, but Charlotte Baker was not. After a time she would call out sharply, her voice carrying through the darkened front room and out the screen door. One word: "ELEANOR!" That was all it took. We knew what she meant; it was midnight, and time for me to leave. Her daughter had to go to work in the morning. We reluctantly unwound and walked to the end of the porch, "two sleepy people in dawn's early light, too much in love to say goodnight." We kissed good-bye, and I made my way home, thinking of nothing else but her.

All too soon, those languid days in Hudson Falls were gone, and I was on my way back to Fairmont.

The Boeing B-29 Superfortress. The biggest, fastest, mightiest heavy bomber built in World War II. Boeing Company Archives

CHAPTER SIX:
THE B-29 SUPERFORTRESS

Some interesting news awaited us upon our return to Fairmont. We were not being assigned to a B-24 or B-17 unit. Instead, we would help form the crews of a new bomber, the B-29 Superfortress. It had been developed secretly and was well suited to the demands of the Pacific theater: long, over-water missions without fighter escorts.

Successor to the famous B-17, the B-29 was the biggest, fastest, mightiest bomber ever made. It had range of 4,100 miles — twice that of a B-17 — could carry twice the bomb load, could fly as high as 32,000 feet, and had an astounding top speed of 358 miles an hour. It was the latest word in man's ability to kill and destroy from on high.

I will never forget my first sight of the silver, streamlined plane as it stood level on double nose and landing wheels on the flight line at Fairmont. Its body was a long, narrow bullet, with a tail that reared three stories into the air. Four 2200-horsepower engines were mounted on the front edge of the wings, each one driving four-bladed propellers that measured seventeen feet from tip to tip. There were two sleek, electrically driven gun turrets on the top, two on the bottom, and one in the tail. The top front turret held four fifty-caliber machine guns; all the others contained two guns. I was awed by the B-29's size and deadly beauty.

Not long after our arrival a second lieutenant led several of us on a tour of the bomber. We climbed up the nose wheel ladder into the front section of the plane to crowd into the area behind the pilot and co-pilot seats. The nose of the bomber, a great round greenhouse, curved ahead of us. The bombardier's position was stepped down from the pilots' level, at the very front. From there he looked down at his target through his Norden bomb sight.

"We're standing in the first of three pressurized cabins in this aircraft," the lieutenant said. "There's this cabin, then the waist cabin, and then the tail compartment. The twenty-nine is the first bomber in the world to be pressurized. What that means is that, at 30,000 feet, the pressure and temperature inside the aircraft will be the same as that at 8,000 feet. You won't need oxygen masks, and you won't need electric long johns to keep warm.

"The front cabin here holds six men — the aircraft commander, the pilot, the bombardier, the flight engineer, the radio operator, and the navigator. It's connected to the pressurized waist section by a tunnel above the bomb bays. We'll be going through the tunnel in a minute. The tail gunner's position is also pressurized, but it's completely separated from the other crew compartments.

"I said no more oxygen masks. What I meant was no more masks during regular flight. Once you get on a high-altitude bomb run, though, you'll have to go onto oxygen in case something hits the aircraft and causes the pressure to drop. The air could go out like a pricked balloon. You'll have to be ready, just in case."

The B-29's predecessors had cold, metal interior skins; we looked about and reached out to touch cabin walls that were covered with green padding. Our new bomber was a joy compared to the narrow, frosty, noisy old B-17s and B-24s in which we had trained.

"A new bomber has to have some new nomenclature," our guide said. "In the B-29 program, the pilot is no longer known as the pilot — he's called the aircraft commander. And what used to be the co-pilot we now call the pilot."

What baloney, I thought. The change seemed quite silly, and I never was able to use the inflated titles. "Pilot" and "co-pilot" did the job quite well. Could that shift have been an early example of the modern practice of softening and obfuscating by coining new names and phrases?

Behind the co-pilot was a floor-to-ceiling bank of instruments that marked the flight engineer's position. The instruments registered the bomber's vital functions: cylinder head temperatures, manifold and oil pressures, the fuel left in the various wing tanks, and other data.

"The beauty of this is that by having a flight engineer watching out for the engines, the AC and the pilot can concentrate on flying," the lieutenant said. "They're busy enough without having to worry about all those other things. On a '17 or a '24, the flight engineer has to man a machine gun; on the '29, all he has to do is watch these dials."

The radio operator's station was just behind the flight engineer, where a big Collins radio sat fastened to a desk. Across the narrow aisle was the navigator's chair, table and lamp. The round base of the upper front turret hung down into the area, much as the bulk of an iceberg lies below the surface of the ocean.

Our guide pointed to a door with a small window at the end of the compartment. Looking through the window, we could see bomb racks on either side of a cavernous bay and another set of racks suspended down the middle.

"Together, this bomb bay and the one behind it can hold 20,000 pounds of bombs — ten tons," he said proudly. "No other bomber in the air today can come close to that, not the Liberator, not the Lancaster, not the Wellington. It's double what a B-17 can carry."

"Let's go into the waist section." He entered the long, padded circular tunnel that ran for forty feet above the bomb bays. He crawled on hands and knees, and we followed behind him.

We emerged into the second pressurized area, a fairly roomy space with a center deck and recessed positions for the waist gunners on either side. Each gunner sat in a seat, looking out of a curved plastic "blister" in his side of the bomber. Mounted on a shelf in front of them were remote-control gun sights, each a foot high.

"Your days of firing a fifty-caliber gun out an open window are long gone," the lieutenant said. "To maintain the pressure inside the aircraft, they've had to place the gun turrets outside the three cabins. They're operated by remote control — through these General Electric sights."

"What if the sights don't work, or if a gun jams?" a gunner asked. "How to you get out there to fix 'em?"

"You don't. This system has tested out beautifully, and is working well in combat. If you do your job right, this equipment will take good care of you."

Cutaway drawing of the B-29, showing its three pressurized compartments and other features. Boeing Company Archives

We had worked with the gun sight in a classroom before our tour of the bomber. I looked through one of them, and flicked the switch that would bring the sight and a turret to life if the plane was in flight. There was a little dial in which the gunner would enter the wing span of an attacking fighter. I turned a circular knob with my left hand that would raise and lower the sight and the turret guns. The sight also could be pivoted to turn the turret from side to side. An intercom switch lay beneath my left thumb.

My right hand held another knob; it adjusted a circle of orange dots that would appear on a view glass at the top of the sight. When an enemy fighter appeared the gunner would enter its wingspan into the sight, look into the view glass, and enclose the plane in the circle. By slowly turning the knob he would widen the ring of dots around the fighter's wing tips as it closed in. A button under my right thumb would fire the guns.

The officer told us that something called an analog computer lay between the gun sights and the turrets. On a mission the flight engineer up front would enter the altitude, wind speed, air speed, temperature, and other factors into the computer. The mechanism would adjust the stream of bullets accordingly. I had no idea what an analog computer was, but it sounded terribly impressive. Today it would be called "state-of-the-art" weaponry.

In the center of the cabin was a pedestal with a chair on the top. Above it was a plastic bubble blister. This was the central fire control gunner's "barber's chair." Seated in it, he could spin about to scan the sky ahead, above and to the sides of the bomber. The CFC man could operate one or more turrets, or assign them to the waist gunners.

"This door obviously leads into the rear bomb bay," said our guide, pointing to an opening identical to the one at the front of the plane. "You can look through here to see if all the bombs have been dropped. This is also a quick way out if you need it — provided the bomb bay doors are open."

Just behind the gunners' area, separated by a full bulkhead, was the windowless radar room. The lieutenant led us through a doorway into the room. The radar operator's position was at a desk in the gloom in front of a circular green screen. When the set was in operation an arm would sweep continually around the screen, illuminating the land forms below. Later on, I came to be fascinated by the way islands and peninsulas glowed momentarily as the arm swung over them.

The radar room was fairly large. It was designed to hold bunk beds for the long flights, but they were never installed. The lower two-thirds of the upper rear gun turret hung down into the room, and a chemical toilet stood in a corner.

We left the radar room by way of a rear door. We stood in a bare, unpadded, unpressurized area. Containers of the ship's oxygen supply were attached to the left wall. Also at the left was the rear entrance door, several feet above the ground, and the ladder that was used to enter and exit the bomber. A gasoline-operated auxiliary generator, called the "putt-putt," stood at the right, below a hatch that opened to the top of the airplane. The generator was needed to help start the engines before take-off, and to provide power for landings. The top of the lower rear turret projected up into the area beyond the putt-putt.

"If any of you want to see what the tail gunner's compartment looks like, go ahead. It won't take long."

I had not yet been assigned a B-29 position, but was curious about the compartment far to the rear of the bomber. I walked ahead for fifteen feet, hunched down to move further as the fuselage narrowed, then dropped to my knees to crawl the remaining distance on the wooden walkway. On either side were long, narrow metal boxes that held coiled belts of ammunition. The belts rolled along tracks that ran beneath the pressurized tail compartment and into the gun turret.

Just ahead was a circular steel door. It opened toward me. I crawled in, closed the door, and stood up in a cubicle just big enough for me to turn around in comfortably. The walls here were also padded.

I shook my head with approval. Compared to the cramped, drafty B-24 ball turret, the tail position on a B-29 was downright spacious.

Behind me was a folded seat that slid up and down on a vertical track. I pulled the seat down and unfolded it. A packed life raft — identical to the one that I would someday use — formed a cushion within the seat frame. To my left was a window, an intercom jack, and an oxygen outlet. At my right was a small oxygen bail-out bottle, and an escape window. A gun sight sat on a narrow ledge in front of me, facing a thick Plexiglas window.

At my feet was another steel door leading into the twin-gun turret. The guns were routinely test-fired at low altitude when the bomber was on its way to a target. If a gun failed to fire at that time the tail gunner could reach it by way of the door. The door remained tightly closed when the compartment was pressurized at higher altitudes. If a machine gun jammed then, the pressure conceivably could be dropped so that the gunner, wearing his oxygen mask, could open the door to work on the weapon. I did not envy him that task in the freezing air.

Having explored the tail compartment, I folded the seat, slid it up, pushed open the door, and made my way back through the

A B-29 tail gunner with his gun sight, pictured without combat equipment and oxygen mask. Boeing Company Archives

unpresssurized area of the airplane. I climbed down the rear entrance ladder to join my companions on the ground.

"That is some airplane," one of them said. "It makes the others look like a piece a junk."

We were standing beneath a formidable weapon. Flying in tight formation, a squadron of B-29s could bring an immense amount of fire-power to bear on attackers. The weapons system was not as dramatic as machine guns fired from open waist windows or a ball turret, but it was far more scientific and effective.

I was so proud of becoming a member of a B-29 crew that my letters home soon were filled with descriptions of the bomber's superior features. I boasted about how high, fast and far the plane could fly, how sleek it was, how many tons of bombs it could carry. After a time, I sensed that my family and friends were growing tired of those enthusiastic reports. Bob Burns wrote that I was becoming known as "B-29 Andy," and I got the message. I remained excited about my assignment, but toned down my letters.

Unknown to us, at the same time that the B-29 had been unveiled in 1943 as a bomber that could fly vast distances without fighter cover, the Eighth Air Force in England had been forced to call a halt to such unescorted missions by its B-17 and B-24 units. The Eighth had been badly mauled by German fighters and anti-aircraft fire on the long flights, losing as many as 20% of its planes in one mission. That ironic fact must have given pause to our military planners: they were announcing a new generation of bombers designed expressly for long-range, unescorted daylight missions at the same time that long-range, unescorted daylight missions against Germany had to be abandoned because they were too costly in men and material.

CHAPTER SEVEN
A Crew is Formed

Until that time, I had served with many different airmen in basic training and at gunnery school. Because we were often assigned alphabetically, most of them had names starting with "D." They had come and gone — a short fellow with the terrible name of Clarence Dangler; kindly Jim Doucette, from Iron Mountain, Michigan; a crazy Russian named Larry Dropkin; and Larry Daniels, a lanky, sad-eyed youth.

Another airman, whose name I have forgotten, was a strapping, happy-go-lucky fellow who liked to look in the latrine mirror and proclaim: "I'm too young and handsome to die."

"If you're counting on your looks to save you, you're in deep shit, my friend," someone replied.

Later, we learned that it was Doucette who had died; the report was that he had stumbled and fallen into a spinning B-29 propeller. It was a grim thought.

The D's had spent their days together, marching, going to classes, exercising, standing inspection, cleaning barracks. We had gone to the mess hall, to the PX, to the base movies, and into town. The juke boxes and films had brought the melancholy wartime songs to us: "Missed the Saturday Dance" ("might have gone, but what for?"), "I'll Walk Alone," "You'll Never Know" ("just how much I love you"), "Sentimental Journey," "Saturday Night is the Loneliest Night of the Week," "Long Ago and Far Away," "I'll be Seeing You" ("in all the old familiar places"), "That's my Desire," and other heart-tugging ballads.

At Fairmont, five officers and six enlisted men were formed into a bomber crew. Our pilot was a big, red-headed Alabaman, Captain Talmadge Heath. He had a gleaming white smile and fuzzy bronze hair on his burly forearms. He shook our hands and looked at us carefully as if to gauge our worth. We found that he was a highly competent pilot — except for one costly incident.

Our first co-pilot was a soft-spoken former teacher, Lieutenant Godsey. For some reason, he was later transferred to another crew. I had the impression that he was too gentle for Captain Heath. Godsey was replaced by a rugged former football player, Lieutenant Charles Mienke. Our navigator, Lieutenant George Walker, was a quiet, congenial officer. Lieutenant Paul Klenk, the bombardier, was short, bald and laconic. Warrant Officer Herbert Kestenbaum was a big, acne-scarred radar man who never let us forget that he was virtually a lieutenant, and thus far superior to the sergeants who lived with him in the rear of the bomber.

The enlisted men, beside myself, were Jim Dudley and Rea Schuessler, waist gunners; Abe Veroba, central fire control gunner; Ken Cox, radioman; and Donald Hutchison, flight engineer. Jim was the soft-spoken Georgian I had met on the troop train en route to Fairmont. Rea was a delightful southerner. He was an older man, possibly twenty-three, thin as a rail, and filled with marvelous anecdotes. Rea had graduated from the University of Alabama and worked in athletic publicity before enlisting. He counseled us about women and other ways of the world.

Abe was from New York City. He was competent, serious and slightly older. Abe kept his distance. He did not concern himself with irrelevant details, such as the names of the volcanic isles on the way to Japan, but he knew exactly what to do when he got there. Ken Cox was a handsome, curly-haired fellow with a bright smile. He had posed for advertisements in Chicago in the past and stands out in our crew photograph. Master Sergeant Hutchison was even older than Rea. We had complete faith in that stocky man's ability as a flight engineer.

I became the tail gunner, probably because I had trained in the isolated B-24 ball turret. It was an assignment that I did not mind at all. The tail compartment was roomier than the ball. It also had its own escape hatch, some armor plate, and a front window of bullet-proof glass. I also liked the idea that I would have a surer shot at a fighter, for his angle of attack would be reduced. He would have a surer shot, too; the added protection testified to that.

The main disadvantage was the isolation from the rest of the crew should I be wounded. The others would have a difficult time getting to me; the ship's pressurization would have to be released and one of them would have to crawl back with a portable oxygen bottle and mask. I decided to worry about that when the time came, if it did.

I never found out why we had been chosen to be B-29 crewmen. The rumor was that we had finished high in our classes and were " '29 material," but possibly it was a random assignment. Whatever the cause, it carried with it an unexpected benefit: had we been assigned to a B-17 or B-24 outfit, we would have been

The crew of "The City of College Park," on Guam, 1945. From top left, Capt. Talmadge Heath, pilot; Lt. Charles Mienke, co-pilot; Lt. George Walker, navigator; Lt. Paul Klenk, bombardier; M Sgt. Donald Hutchison, flight engineer. Bottom row, from left, the author; Tech Sgt. Abe Veroba, central fire control gunner; Staff Sgt. Donald Cox, radioman; Staff Sgt. Jim Dudley, right waist gunner; and Staff Sgt. Rea Schuessler, left waist gunner. Warrant Officer Herbert Kestenbaum, radar operator, is not pictured.

shipped out with little delay. Instead, the Superfort training would keep us in the country for additional months. It was not something we sought or desired. It was simply the way it turned out.

We became a cohesive crew in long training flights across the Midwest. There were not enough B-29s to go around, so we often flew in B-17s. I spent hours looking down through a hatch at the fields and farmhouses and villages, wondering who lived there, what their lives were like, and where their sons were that day.

We learned to get along socially, as well, especially the enlisted men. We would go into Lincoln or Omaha, rent a hotel room, and drink limited amounts of hard liquor. Jim Dudley and I hitch-hiked to Lincoln one day. A traveling salesman picked us up, and I was surprised to hear him say how disgusted he was that so many young men were being thrown into the war.

The officers often found women to join us on our forays into Omaha. Someone on the crew liked to sing, and taught us to harmonize. We sang far into the night, oblivious to those in adjoining rooms. After all, there was a war on.

Although married, Captain Heath started seeing an attractive young woman whose husband was overseas. She was slim and appealing. While we were singing one night, she came to my side. She stood close and smiled at me as we harmonized.

"You sing well," she said. "Where did you learn?"

"It just came to me. Harmonizing's fun."

"Did you sing back home?"

"No, not really."

"And where would that be?" she asked.

"Where would what be?"

"Home. Where are you from?"

"Upstate New York. A place called Hudson Falls. Fifty-two miles above Albany on the Vermont border."

"Do you miss it?"

"Sure."

"And your girl friend?"

"Yes. I sure do."

"How much?" she asked, looking at me closely.

"A lot," I said.

"I can see why she likes you," she said. "You're cute." I didn't know what to say.

"Thank you."

We sang more songs, sipped our drinks, and talked. After a time she looked up at me. "You know, it's getting too noisy in here. I wonder if we could find a place that's a little quieter."

I was speechless again. I didn't know what she meant. Where would we go, and why? How would I get back to the base? What would Captain Heath think? I knew he would be furious, and no doubt would have me dropped from our airplane with our next load of practice bombs if I made off with his girl friend. I let her invitation pass and she later returned to the captain's side. The truth was that I was too timid to take such a bold step.

Years later, I wondered if Captain Heath had suggested that she approach me in that way. His sense of humor had an almost sadistic edge. Or did she tire of him and decide instead to initiate a young airman before he flew off to war?

Longer flights began in old, over-worked B-29s. It was then that we discovered that, for all its advertised virtues, the plane had a major defect — its Wright R-3350 engines were highly temperamental. They were hard to cool inside their streamlined nacelles, frequently overheated, and were quick to catch fire. Magnesium was used in the engines to make them lighter, but the metal burned fiercely if ignited. If not contained, the fire could burn through to the main wing spars. The engines became known as "Wrongs." Every take-off at full power was a time of danger. During flight the waist gunners watched the engines for signs of sparks, smoke or leaking oil. Whenever the intercom clicked on during a long journey, every member of the crew perked up to hear if an observer was reporting a possible problem.

If that were not enough, B-29 engines also could gulp gas at a prodigious rate — something on the order of five gallons a minute. If the flight engineer did not set up precise cruise controls, he could find his fuel gauges dropping alarmingly fast. Early in the B-29 program, planes that left on practice flights from air fields in the Midwest to "bomb" Havana, Cuba often were forced to land one or two states short of their homes bases on their return trips — even without a load of explosives.

We were dropping off to sleep one night in our barracks when the mechanics on a nearby flight line began testing the B-29 engines on which they had been working. As the mechanics fed more gas, the roar became louder and louder until it was a steady drone.

"The good thing about this," said a dry voice from the darkness, "is that those engines can't keep it up very long."

The problem came home on our simulated run to Havana. It was a long flight, much of it over water to the island, thus simulating what lay ahead in the Pacific. When we were well out over the Gulf of Mexico, the intercom clicked.

"Right waist to Captain — we've got some oil coming off number three."

"Where? How much? Any smoke?"

"No smoke. The oil's off the top — there's a stream coming down the wing."

"Okay. We've got it."

Eventually the engine had to be shut down and the propeller blades "feathered" — stilled and turned edgewise into the wind. An hour later, another engine began smoking. It, too, had to be stopped. To make matters worse, Captain Heath soon had to reduce power on a third engine. We began to lose altitude rapidly. Our pilot radioed ahead for a "straight-in" landing at Batista air base, without an approach pattern. Over the island, he opened the bomb bays. We put on our parachutes and looked down at the green fields, ready to jump if given the order.

Realizing he could reach the landing strip, Captain Heath closed the bomb bays and told us to get into our crash positions. Abe, Herb and I braced against the rear bomb bay bulkhead, holding the backs of our heads with our hands as Jim and Rea sat in their recessed seats.

"This will do us as about as much good as a fly tightening his muscles before the swatter hits," I said. No one replied as we dropped lower.

Unfortunately, the runway was being repaired and the Cuban tower had failed to notify everyone on the ground. A truck was crossing as we approached. The driver saw us coming, jumped out, and ran. Captain Heath slammed on the right brakes, gunned what power remained in the left engines, and we swerved sharply to the

Trouble aboard a B-29 as oil leaks within a hot engine.

right. The left wing flattened the truck down to its chassis. We bumped and skidded wildly into a field as the landing gear collapsed beneath us. We scrambled to the rear door, and stepped onto the ground without a ladder. We ran from the plane as fast as we could, fearing an explosion that never came. Breathing heavily from excitement and exertion, we looked back at our stricken bomber.

After a lengthy debriefing, we were given passes to visit Havana. Our bus to the city was filled with Cubans. There was hostility in the air as they watched us. I was surprised; I saw ourselves leaving our homes and risking our lives to defend their freedom, but apparently they viewed us as damn Yankee intruders. We went to a half-empty night club, tasted rum for the first time, and returned to the base. The next day, a B-17 flew us to Ft. Myers, Florida, then back to our base.

Before the engines had begun acting up on our way to Cuba, I had written a poem called "The Twenty-nine Twitch." It read:

> You've heard of the heebie-jeebies,
> The four and the seven-year itch.
> But worst of all, you'll someday recall,
> Is a plague dubbed the Twenty-nine Twitch.
>
> St. Vitus Dance and ants-in-the-pants
> Have been, I'm told, well cured.
> But this malady of ours
> Is increased through the hours,
> Forever to be endured.
>
> An endless array of troubles all day
> Is the deal that fate has in store.
> For you men in the news — your '29 crews —
> It's rough, this Army Air Corps.
>
> In the sky we feed on fine meals, indeed,
> And loaf in soft, easy chairs,
> Read books and rest, it's life at it's best,
> Flying's all comfort, no cares.
>
> That's what they say in the papers each day
> About a bird that soars with such ease.
> But tell an inmate who's flown in the crate —
> And stand back - give him air - if you please.
>
> Oil tubes, buffer tubes, relief tubes,
> Sandwiches, servos, and stowing.
> Headspace, livingspace, floorspace,
> And the list keeps on growing and growing.
>
> So we know it well, this high-flying hell,
> And our hands and our knees are unsteady.
> Our eyes are crossed, and our sanity lost —
> You know, Hap, we'll never be ready.

Hap was General Hap Arnold, head of the U.S. Air Force. Rea asked me for the poem, and took it to the base newspaper. When it appeared in print, a subtle bit of censorship had taken place. The final line had been altered to read:

"You know, Hap, we'll *always* be ready." A diligent staffer had seen fit to protect us all from the wrath of a four-star general.

On another occasion, we landed at Lake Charles, Louisiana and caused a local sensation. B-29 crews were adept at finding ways to be "forced" to make unscheduled landings at interesting bases for "mechanical reasons." Just in case, the crews often carried with them fresh uniforms and tooth brushes. Lake Charles had never seen a B-29 before. People at the base came out of their buildings to look at the big silver bird, squatting far across the field. Guards were posted around our bomber, with orders not to let anyone enter the aircraft. We cleaned up, and went into town for a crew party.

Women mysteriously appeared at our table. Our officers had spread the word that base secretaries would be welcome to join us, and some of them did. The wore their best dresses and silk stockings. We sat around a table, drinking beer and talking. Ken Cox had a girl at his side who conveyed that unmistakable virginal look. ("It takes one to know one," he told me afterward.) After a time, the two of them moved down to my end of the table, where Rea was telling me about Alabama's superior football teams. I had a clear impression that Ken was unloading his date on us, for he sat her down nearby and soon disappeared. We didn't mind; we talked with her about her secretarial duties and life in Lake Charles until it was time to return to the base.

When we were trucked out to our bomber the next morning, a stocky black Army private stood in front of the plane. He held his rifle high and across his body, blocking our way.

"Halt!" he cried.

"Halt?" Captain Heath said. "What do you mean, halt? This is *my* airplane!" He was furious.

"Ah's sorry, sir, but my orders is that nobody get in."

Captain Heath, iron-willed southerner that he was, raged at the man, demanding his name and serial number, and telling him he was going to be reported to his commanding officer. But the soldier remained firm.

"Ah's sorry, sir," he kept repeating. I felt pity for him, and admired his stand. He was being absurd, but he was following his orders to the letter, and should not be blamed. I stood directly behind the captain and kept winking and nodding at the soldier to let him know we did not all feel the same way as our pilot. Someone radioed the control tower and an officer came out to tell the soldier we could enter. We boarded the plane and took off.

Later that fall, we were transferred to Clovis, New Mexico. We were there a month, then sent to the end of the world — the Rattlesnake Air Force Base at Pyote, Texas. Pyote was a tiny town set in the sagebrush country of the Texas panhandle. It was 150 miles east of El Paso, and 250 miles west of Abiline. In between were exotic places such as Monahans, Big Springs, Pecos, Sweetwater, and Odessa. We visited some of them on Saturday nights and flew over them routinely on training flights.

I came to the conclusion that the beauty of the Women's Army Corps members at a given air base was inversely proportional to the base's distance from major urban centers. The women at Pyote were ancient crones — perhaps thirty-five years old. We drank beer with two of them in a very dim Monahans bar one night, only to be embarrassed when we encountered them in full daylight on the base the next day. They actually had wrinkles at the corners of their eyes.

Those trips into town were quite tame; no wild, drunken orgies, nor moments of romance for men about to fly off into the great unknown. Few of us knew how to drink, and the local towns were swamped with other servicemen. Even if there had been women available, many of us would not have known how to approach them. So we would find a crowded saloon, order a Coke and the only liquor around — something called PM — and sip it down with little pleasure.

I stood at a bar one night, having a beer and feeling quite worldly with my Air Force shoulder patch, new sergeant's stripes, silver gunner's wings and the utterly common Good Conduct, Marksman and American Theater ribbons on my chest. A stocky woman seated nearby turned to me.

"Can I ask you a question?"

"Sure."

"I've been watching in the mirror — why do you make such a face every time you take a drink of your beer?"

I was hurt. I had never drunk beer before, and did not like the taste of the stuff. But a buck sergeant could not be expected to sip lemonade.

Looking back, I realize that there were no radios in our lives, no tape decks, no television, few cameras, and no telephone calls. The barracks contained only the noises of men — laughing, griping, joking, talking. Ken Cox had the one camera and is responsible for the crew photos I have today. As for long distance phone calls home, very few single enlisted men made them. I never did; I had grown up without a telephone in our house, so the process seemed to be complicated, unnatural, and expensive. Separation from family and friends in those days was quite complete, with letters the only link. How unlike the minute-by-minute coverage of America's modern televised wars, featuring live interviews with generals, fighter-bomber pilots, tank corps sergeants, and female supply depot privates.

Not long after we arrived at Pyote, a letter from Chuck arrived. My brother was stationed in the infantry replacement training center at Camp Blanding, Florida, along with 40,000 other men. He was nearing the end of his stay at "the largest training camp in the United States, and possibly in the world." Soon he would be sent overseas. As part of his training, he and his fellow riflemen had to crawl on their bellies beneath low wires as live ammunition flew close overhead. It was a frightening exercise. Chuck strongly hinted that he would not mind being transferred into the Air Force instead of going to Europe with the infantry.

"There's a regulation that twin brothers can be together in the same unit if one of them requests it," he wrote. "Some guy in our outfit who has a brother in the Navy just got transferred out of this rathole. Lucky bastard. Not a bad idea if you ask me." He signed his letter with the words, "I'll see you in '52."

I didn't follow up on his suggestion, thinking that it was far too late for the change to be made. The war would be over by the time the paperwork was done. Deep inside, I knew that was not the full story; I enjoyed my independence in my own branch of service.

As the 1944 holiday season approached we heard "I'll Be Home For Christmas" being played unendingly on the PX juke box. We dreamed of that, but spent the holidays in Pyote instead. Late in January our furloughs came through. Our orders were to report in two weeks to the overseas staging base at Hastings, Nebraska.

A day of our leave was required to cross Texas by train. We went on to Chicago, Buffalo, and Albany. The cars were jammed with servicemen: marines in trim green uniforms, sailors in floppy pants with funny rows of buttons, soldiers wearing marksman medals and division insignias on their khaki jackets, airmen with silver wings on their chests. We filled up the seats, sat on luggage in the aisles, and hung about the lounge areas and dining cars. There was a spirit of conviviality in the air. I don't remember a single argument or fight. The youth of the nation was under arms, and on the move. And many of us were headed home on leave.

My arrival in Albany is still fresh in my mind, as is the walk into the cold night and down a dark street to the Adirondack Bus Lines depot. There I boarded a warm bus for the trip to Glens Falls. The familiar three-mile journey to Hudson Falls followed; I got off at Maple Street and once again carried my bags out to Coombs Avenue. I was greeted by my parents and cousin with broad smiles, and lost no time calling Bake.

Once again, the two weeks vanished in a flurry of visits, movies, high school basketball games, and trips to the drug store. I picked up Bake at her house on those frosty evenings, and we walked briskly down Mechanic Street to the corner of Main Street to catch the bus to Glens Falls. The bus was crowded, its windows coated with steam or frost. A man gave up his seat to Bake and I stood proudly beside her in the aisle, swaying slightly as I held onto an overhead strap. As the bus moved along its lights showed high snow banks on either side of the road and dark clusters of people waiting in the cold at the bus stops ahead. We were on our way to Glens Falls to see *Since You Went Away* at the Paramount theater. It starred Jennifer Jones and Robert Walker as young lovers in wartime. Bake and I held hands in the darkened theater and identified with the two characters.

We ended the evening in the Baker family's warm front room, where we waited for her parents to go to bed after we had finished our ice cream ritual. When they were gone, Bake sat on my lap in a large, blue easy chair. Soft dance music, broadcast late at night from a hotel in New York City, formed a romantic backdrop. We kept the radio low so that we would not disturb her parents beyond their closed door. But after a time, Mrs. Baker's call emerged: "Eleanor!" Once again it was time for me to leave. I walked home in my heavy overcoat, cupping my ears in the cold, running to slide across patches of ice in the street.

War novels and movies often describe how young lovers are overcome by their passions the night before the soldier, sailor or airman goes off to battle, but that did not happen to us. Our standards — and respect for each other — remained high.

The farewells this time were much harder, for we all knew I was going overseas. Again I left Bake early the night before departing, and went through the routine of packing with my parents watching. Ken Howe drove us, Agnes and Bake to Albany in a Buick that held three people in the front seat. Mom, Bake and I sat in the back. It was a sad ride, but we tried to be cheerful, talking about anything but the future.

Standing on the slushy pavement in front of the railroad station, we said good-bye. I hugged Mom and shook Dad's hand. He had been taking nitroglycerin tablets for an angina problem for years and puffed after the slightest effort. I looked into his eyes and wondered if I would ever see him again; I imagined him wondering the same about me.

Dad was not given to long statements. "Take care of yourself," he said. "I will — you, too." We did not embrace, for men did not do such things in those days. I wish I had, for I never saw him again. I gave Bake a brief kiss, picked up my bags, and disappeared into the station.

North Field, Guam. 1945. Home of the 314th Wing of the 20th Air force. Japan lies straight ahead, 1600 miles and more than seven hours away. J. R. Eyerman, LIFE Magazine, ©Time Inc.

CHAPTER EIGHT
INTO COMBAT

Reunited in Hastings, Nebraska after our leaves, our crew received overseas shots and bundles of new equipment. We also took possession of a shiny B-29, fresh off the Boeing production line at Renton, Washington. The plane had the unforgettable smell of hydraulic fluid, electrical equipment, gasoline, and a spotless new interior. We looked it over from top to bottom, then adjourned to a quiet crew party in Greater Downtown Hastings.

Captain Heath's wife joined us there to say good-bye. She was a sweet southern woman.

A few days later we flew to Mather Field near Sacramento, California. A bus took the enlisted men into San Francisco that night through a heavy fog. The officers preceded us in their own bus. Once we arrived, Abe and Hutch went their separate ways. I could imagine Abe going to a museum, an art gallery or a synagogue, while Hutch headed for a bar. Our flight engineer was older and rougher than the rest of us, and probably searched out other adventures. Abe and Hutch never told us where they went, or what they had done. They were more mature; we were green kids.

Jim, Rea, Ken and I found our way to the ground floor bar of the Sir Francis Drake hotel, and spent the evening there. We didn't know what else to do. It was our last fling before going overseas. We sat at a table and drank beer in a room filled with other servicemen. It was not at all like the Hollywood scenes of Navy and Air Force officers having a farewell drink at the bar at the top of the Mark Hopkins Hotel, surrounded by beautiful women.

On March 14, 1945, we took off from Mather, followed the Sacramento River to San Francisco Bay, then flew out over the Golden Gate Bridge. We were a lone airplane in a gray sky, headed for war. I cannot look at the bridge today without remembering that flight, and the nineteen-year-old boy seated in the tail, watching the city and the continent fade from sight. San Francisco was a cluster of low, white buildings on the hills, with only a few tall structures to be seen.

Twelve hours later, the intercom clicked. "Hawaii ahead," Captain Heath announced. George Walker had aimed us straight toward Diamond Head, near Waikiki Beach. As the plane banked to the left, we crowded around Jim's side blister to catch our first glimpse of the islands. We had left drab winter landscapes behind, and were stunned by the brilliant tropical beauty. I was amazed by the vivid blues and greens, the snow-white surf and the lush mountains.

"That's a beautiful sight," someone said.

"Yeah - why don't we just stay here for a while?"

"We could learn to do the hula dance."

"Or at least watch it."

"Now you're talking."

We coasted past Waikiki and Honolulu, and on by Pearl Harbor, where the battleships Arizona and West Virginia lay submerged at their berths, with thousands of men entombed inside — among them a sailor from Hudson Falls. Scattered across the harbor was an incredible array of naval vessels. We circled to land at Rogers Field, where buildings still bore the scars of Japanese strafing four years earlier.

We did stay a while in Hawaii: Captain Heath had a prostate problem, and had to be hospitalized for a few days. Prostate was a word I had never heard before, but I appreciated the fact that it would give us extra time to look around. We were told not to reveal our whereabouts in letters home, so we didn't — but I wrote on flimsy air mail paper with a hula girl superimposed on it. Jim, Rea and I went into downtown Honolulu. The streets were rolling seas of white sailor uniforms and army khaki. Another day we hitchhiked a ride in a jeep driven by an Army chaplain; he took us across pineapple fields to the north shore of the island, along a coastal road, and back over a spectacular pass above the city.

The next morning we took off on a ten-hour flight to Kwajalein. The island had been taken from the Japanese a year before after a difficult fight. The palm trees were still shredded from the bombardment, and destroyed equipment lay rusting in the lagoon. We landed safely on the short airstrip that Army troops had made possible, and slept soundly between clean sheets. The sacrifices of the soldiers had cleared the way for those who followed.

After another long flight, we neared the island of Guam, the southernmost of the three Marianas Islands. I went to the nose of the plane to watch. As we approached I could see once again how the full resources of an angry nation had been marshaled against Japan. The harbor at Agana was alive with warships. Farther north vast fields overflowed with tanks, trucks, artillery, and other war materiel. Further on, acres of tents housed a Marine Corps division resting up for the final assault on the Japanese home islands.

North Field had been bulldozed out of the jungle by Navy Seabees as soon as the island had been secured by the Army and Marines the previous fall. The thick growth had been shoved into long rows in a round-the-clock operation. A mammoth asphalt runway was laid down, taxi strips and revetments — paved cul de sacs that held one or two bombers each — were formed. Company streets were created and other areas were cleared for a mess hall, a large briefing tent, and Quonset huts.

The capture of the Marianas — Guam, Saipan and Tinian — was one of the major events of the Pacific war. It brought the Japanese homeland within the range of B-29s flying from islands that could easily be supplied by sea. The earliest Superfort squadrons had been based in China, but could fly only a few missions a month because their fuel and bombs had to be laboriously transported from India over the Himalayas.

We landed between rain squalls and taxied to a hardstand past dozens of B-29s bearing yellow M's, P's, O's and K's in big black squares on their tall tails. They were members of the 314th Wing of the 20th Air Force. Each letter represented a bombardment group within the wing. Each group contained three squadrons, and each squadron was made up of fifteen aircraft.

We were joining the M's — the famous 19th Bombardment Group. The 19th had nearly been wiped out as a B-17 unit at Clark

Field in the Philippines the day after Pearl Harbor. It had been withdrawn to Australia, then was returned home to be reconstituted as a B-29 outfit. We were assigned to the 93rd Squadron, a unit that traced its roots back even further, to the Lafayette Escadrille in the first World War. Colin Kelly, the Congressional Medal of Honor winner who died early in World War II trying to sink a Japanese battleship, had been a member of the 93rd.

As we unloaded our equipment and boarded a truck, I wondered what had become of the B-29 whose place we had taken. We soon found out. The 19th Bombardment Group had arrived a few weeks earlier, in time to take part in the first low-level fire raid on Tokyo on March 9. The group was still stunned by its losses that night — three bombers shot down, including two from the 93rd squadron. The squadron's commanding officer and operations officer were among those lost.

The 20th Air Force fire raids had continued every second night against Nagoya, Osaka, and Kobe before we arrived. When the missions were over, thirty square miles of those cities had been laid waste in a nine-day period. A total of twenty-one B-29s had failed to return. Our bomber stood where one of those planes had rested.

My earliest impressions of our new home were of jungle, rain and mud. We lived in tents surrounded by high rows of uprooted trees and got about on wooden walkways. After a few weeks we moved into newly-constructed Quonset huts that were high and dry.

Not long after we arrived Captain Heath and Lieutenant Mienke went on a mission to Japan as observers. They were strangely noncommittal when they came back.

"What was it like?" I asked Mienke a day later.

"It was interesting. Spectacular. You'll find out soon enough."

Our turn came not long afterward. On March 30 we were alerted for our first raid. We made our way to the briefing tent that was filled with combat crews sprawled on rows of benches. At the front was a huge map. The Marianas were at the bottom. Iwo Jima was halfway up, and the Japanese homeland angled across the top, 1600 miles away.

A red string led from our base straight to Nagoya, on the main island of Honshu. It was to be a high-altitude daylight mission against the Mitsubishi aircraft engine factory, one of the two largest engine plants in Japan. It was a heavily-defended target that previous missions had failed to destroy. Briefing officers told us about the importance of the complex. We listened closely to reports about the weather, the location of enemy antiaircraft batteries, the positions of rescue submarines and aircraft, the tactics of Japanese fighter planes, and other details. A chaplain concluded the session with a short prayer. We sat with heads bowed.

We gathered up our parachute harnesses, parachutes, inflatable Mae Wests, survival vests, helmets, oxygen masks, hunting knives, sunglasses and other items, and climbed into a truck with benches along each side. There was little talk in the darkness as we rode to our hardstand.

Much to our disappointment, the new bomber we had flown to Guam had been taken away from us and assigned to a more veteran crew. We inherited an older plane, No. 43-92996, and unloaded in front of it. We climbed aboard to check our equipment and positions, then returned to sit on the pavement near the front landing gear, our backs against the big wheels.

A long hour later, it was time to go. We paired up to pull the big propeller blades down and through, twelve turns per blade, to make certain that no oil had accumulated in the lower cylinder heads. I climbed up the rear ladder and started the auxiliary generator.

"Putt-putt started and on line," I reported.

"Roger," Captain Heath replied. The men up front closed the bomb bays and switched on the first engine. The propellers slowly began to turn. The engine coughed to life, spewed smoke, and settled into a steady roar. Three other engines followed in turn.

Few wartime scenes can be more dramatic than dozens of heavy bombers departing on a mission. I will never forget the sight. One at a time, on a precise schedule, the B-29s inched out of their paved revetments and fell into line, brakes screeching, high tails bobbing in the moonlight like some prehistoric monsters. Nose to tail, the bombers edged ahead in a slow parade to the head of the runway. The air was filled with noise and fumes.

The large flaps at the back edge of our wings were slowly extended as we moved ahead, adding a fifth more surface area to the bomber's narrow wings. The flaps allowed take-offs and landings at lower speeds.

A dramatic moment as 314th wing bombers line up on Guam for a strike against Japan. Boeing Company Archives

"Left flap, twenty-five degrees," Rea reported to the pilot. "Right flap, twenty-five degrees," Jim added.

A wooden control tower lay ahead, to the right of the runway. Red and green lights from the tower triggered a take-off every minute. When the green light flashed, Captain Heath opened the engines to full power and stood on the brakes, holding us fast as the engines roared. He released the brakes, and we began lumbering down the long runway. It was a dangerous moment, with little margin of safety; the temperamental engines had to haul a thirty-five-ton bomber, four tons of bombs, eight thousand gallons of gasoline, thousands of rounds of ammunition, and eleven men into the air.

We slowly picked up speed, engines roaring, wisps of vapor trailing from opened engine cowlings that reminded me of the laid-back ears of a running dog. We seemed to hug the ground forever. Captain Heath held the nose down to gain as much speed as possible, then eased us into the air. He touched the brakes briefly to stop the wheels from spinning once we were airborne.

Mienke quickly retracted the wheels into the inboard engine nacelles to rid ourselves of the air resistance. "Gear up," he said. We sagged over the rocky headlands at the end of the island, adding speed as we dropped. Heath "milked" the flaps back into the wings as we sped on.

Seated in the tail, I watched the bombers behind us, the runway, the cliffs and the island disappear. We were on our way. After a time I test-fired my guns, went back through the unpressurized section to turn off the putt-putt, and joined the others in the waist compartment for the long trip. We had left at three in the morning to reach our target seven hours later. That timing would give us several hours of daylight for our return to Guam after the bomb run.

Three and one-half hours later we passed over Iwo Jima, a brown pork-chop-shaped island halfway to Japan. Marines had taken it from the Japanese only a few weeks earlier after a monumental battle. The island's new landing strip, built while the fighting still raged, already was a welcome haven for bombers in distress.

Although the B-29's top speed was 358 miles an hour, it actually was flown more slowly when loaded with bombs and gas, and when a long trip lay ahead. The average indicated airspeed was closer to 220 miles an hour, which meant that the crews had to spend more than fifteen and one-half hours in the air on every mission. The trip from Guam to Japan and back covered some 3,200 miles.

Three hours after we passed over Iwo, Captain Heath announced that he was starting the climb to our bombing altitude of 25,000 feet. I returned to the tail and settled in. Ahead of us a lead bomber, its nose wheel extended for identification, circled above a tiny volcanic island off the coast of Japan. Arriving B-29s cut across the wide circle to catch up to the leader and other bombers. We edged into a formation of twelve planes. Once we had assembled we joined 256 Superforts in a long bomber stream, headed for Nagoya.

The side windows of my tail compartment flared out slightly. I could crane my head around to see the wings and engines. Looking down, I saw the coast of Japan appear beneath a wing. The enemy territory appeared dark and foreboding. There was no turning back. We were being drawn inexorably toward a point high in the sky above Japan's second-largest city.

My stomach was tight as we continued on and turned into our bomb run. We were flying in close formation, keeping each other company as we maximized our fire power and bombing pattern. One B-29 was just behind and below our plane, only yards away. I looked into the front cabin, where the bombardier, pilot and co-pilot were hunched tensely in their flak suits, oxygen masks and helmets.

I kept my guns angled straight up in the air, knowing that the men in the following bombers were frightened by friendly weapons pointed in their direction.

It was quiet in our bomber as we bore ahead in perfect weather. The first puffs of antiaircraft fire began to appear. I strained to watch in every direction for enemy aircraft.

"Twelve o'clock level," Mienke shouted, and the guns chattered up front. A Japanese fighter flashed through our formation, the pilot's head swiveling as he looked about. I fired as soon as I could without hitting any bombers behind us. Someone had hit him - I hadn't - and he bailed out. He drifted to earth far to the rear.

As we neared the target area, the antiaircraft fire increased. Our introduction to the war was a sky filled with ugly black bursts of fire, each burst sending jagged bits of steel flying in all directions.

I tried to shrink my body into the smallest possible target. The deadly puffs contrasted with the long, almost beautiful white tentacles of phosphorous bombs that were dropped into our formation by a Japanese plane flying above us. It was a surrealistic scene. Several bursts walked silently in a line toward our plane, but stopped short. Out of range to our right, a twin-engine Japanese fighter radioed our speed and altitude to the ground batteries.

I was struck by the unreality of it all, although nothing could be more real. Perhaps all warriors are somewhat traumatized by their situations. We were in the thick of it, five miles above Japan, and yet I was observing myself and our situation almost with detachment. The cool interior of my compartment, the gleaming bombers all about us, the clear air outside, the vicious bursts of flak, the masked and helmeted men huddled in the plane close behind, all seemed from another world.

We were suspended in time on a steady bomb run from which we could not deviate. Flak described as "intense and accurate" crashed all about us. Finally Paul Klenk called out "bombs away" and our plane surged upward, relieved of its burden. Looking around, I saw schools of fat, five-hundred pound bombs drop from the other bombers and begin their long slants to earth; looking down moments later, I could see explosions twinkling in the target area, much like strings of tiny Chinese firecrackers.

Our formation wheeled into a long turn to head back home. Off the coast, the individual bombers spread out to begin their solitary flights to Guam. The feeling of relief in our B-29 was palpable.

"My," Rea said. "That was quite a party."

"Only thirty-four more to go," Cox added. No one answered.

Post-strike photos showed "excellent" results; the *New York Times* reported the next day that the target had been hit squarely by our bombs, resulting in the "virtually total destruction of the vast works." All but twenty-four of the 140 buildings were destroyed — some 3,446,000 square feet of roof space.

The antiaircraft fire was "the heaviest yet encountered," according to the reports of veteran crew members, and fighter opposition was severe. Five aircraft were lost and more than half the bombers were damaged by flak, but I did not see any Superforts go down.

"Look what you did to my airplane," our ground crew chief said after we landed and returned to our revetment. He mounted a ladder to poke the end of a screwdriver into one of the small holes that had been created by bits of flak on the underside of our right wing.

"Sorry about that," said Captain Heath.

If the bombing run over Nagoya seemed interminable, the next one seemed even longer. It came over Tokyo on April 13, during the second low-level incendiary raid on that city.

Although our high-altitude Nagoya mission had been successful, earlier precision bombing from that height had been largely ineffective because of the dense clouds and strong winds above Japan. Clear weather was found over the target only four to seven days a month. General Curtis LeMay, head of the 20th Air Force, concluded that individual B-29s, flying in at five to eight thousand feet at night, would be far more accurate than if they bombed from 25,000 to 30,000 feet. They could burn out large areas of the Japanese cities, "de-house" the population and destroy the many cottage industries that supported the war effort.

Another major advantage was that the bombers would not have to make the long, demanding climb to high altitude that strained the engines and drank up fuel. Nor would they have to assemble in formation and jockey about on the way to the target. Consequently, they could carry twice the bomb load. Engine maintenance would be reduced, which would result in more bombers over the target.

LeMay's decision had dismayed the B-29 crews. The low-level raids obviously were much closer to ground antiaircraft and searchlight batteries, and left less room for crewmen to bail out if their plane was shot down. Many B-29s were seen to catch fire, explode, and plunge to earth. The incendiary raids against major cities were not welcomed by the airmen.

We took off late in the afternoon on a mission appropriately code-named "Perdition" — Hell, utter destruction, entire loss, ruin. Our target was the Arsenal area of the city, six miles northwest of the Imperial Palace. It was a sector that contained housing and factories that made or stored machine guns, artillery, bombs, and other arms. An estimated 30,000 to 80,000 people lived in every square mile of that area.

Each of the 348 bombers carried between five and eight tons of incendiary bombs, depending upon the distance they had to fly.

Guam was 125 miles south of Saipan, so our ground crew loaded fewer bombs and more fuel. Each of our main bombs contained a cluster of fifty-five smaller bombs filled with jellied gasoline; the big bombs opened at 5,000 feet to scatter the smaller ones. One bomber could create a flaming swath a half-mile wide and a mile and a half long.

As we flew north that night, we heard on our headsets that President Roosevelt had died suddenly while vacationing in Georgia. The news shocked us, for we were fond of our president and respected his steady leadership. We buzzed about the development for a time, speculating about the little-known vice president, Harry Truman, who now would move into the White House. We put the news behind us and concentrated again on the mission ahead.

We arrived off the coast at midnight. Looking ahead, I could see the glow of the burning city. We had heard about the three hundred antiaircraft guns awaiting us, and were fearful. The report was that bombers caught in the searchlight beams above the city often were "goners."

"This is it," someone said as we bore ahead.

"Stay off the intercom," Captain Heath ordered.

Once over the city, I looked down into an indescribable scene. Tokyo was an inferno. Block after block of buildings were aflame. The fire covered eleven square miles of the city, and smoke towered thousands of feet into the air. The smell of burning wood and other materials came through our open bomb bays. A violent updraft suddenly drove us hundreds of feet higher, pinning us to our seats. I could hardly lift my hand.

Searchlights swept the sky and tracer fire laced through the night. I strained to watch for other bombers and Japanese night fighters. A few thousand feet above us, and to the rear, I saw a silver bomber caught by the searchlight beams. It shone brightly in the night sky. Bombs began tumbling down from its open bays, shimmering in the light of the fires and the beams.

Suddenly a beam fastened on our own bomber. It was quickly joined by others. It was bright enough inside my compartment to read a newspaper. I felt naked in the grip of the beams as we plunged wildly ahead, waiting for our load of bombs to be dropped. They finally fell free, and Captain Heath nosed the plane down to gain speed.

"Let's get the hell out of here," he said as he banked swiftly down and away. We were greatly relieved as we headed home. More than one hundred miles from the city, I could still see the red glow in the sky. Beneath that glow, thousands of people were dead or dying.

Some 2,100 tons of bombs fell on Tokyo that night. "B-29's Set Great Tokyo Fires; Explosions Heard 100 Miles," the *Times* reported afterward. A correspondent who flew in a 314th Wing bomber wrote: "A very large task force of B-29s swarmed over Tokyo, a minute apart, in the darkness early today with millions of pounds of incendiaries. From my vantage point in this battleship of the sky, it appeared that the Army Air Force had achieved its goal of wiping out the fireable sections of the Japanese capital. The sight of the capital aflame would thrill any American, and it was especially exciting for me, making my first combat mission in the Pacific air theater."

Seven bombers and seventy-seven men failed to return. Our crew had emerged shaken, but unscathed.

The invasion of Okinawa had begun on April 1. American warships standing off the island were taking heavy losses from Japan's "secret weapon" — the Divine Wind Special Attack Force, otherwise known as the Kamikazes. A "divine wind" had driven Mongol hordes from an intended invasion of Japan in the 13th Century; the Japanese believed that thousands of suicide pilots could similarly save the nation in 1945. Nearly 4,000 Japanese pilots, mostly between eighteen and twenty-four, gave their lives to the cause. In all, they sank thirty-eight ships and killed 5,000 American and British sailors off Okinawa — more than died at Pearl Harbor. The battle at sea alone had been the bloodiest in American naval history.

The Kamikazes became such a serious threat to the Navy that the 20th Air Force was diverted from its strategic bombing and fire raids to attack the home bases of the suicide planes in southern Japan. Two thousand individual flights against seventeen airfields on Kyushu were flown over the next three weeks. The bases were hit almost daily during April against opposition that ranged from weak to ferocious. We took part in those missions, dropping fragmentation and heavy demolition bombs onto the runways, hangers and repair shops at Kanoya, Nittagahara, Kokubu, Chiran, and

Ibusuki. The missions were not particularly difficult for our squadron, although each was wearying and had its moments of danger. Other groups were met by swarms of enemy fighters.

I remember looking down on peaceful Japanese villages as we headed toward one of our targets in southern Japan. Just as I had wondered about the families who had lived in the farm homes beneath our practice flights over the Midwest, I speculated now on those living below us in rural Japan and where and how their sons might be serving their emperor.

After the raids on the southern airfields we returned to industrial targets in a campaign to knock out Japan's military capabilities. On May 11, 400 bombers were sent to the Kawanishi aircraft company factory, between the cities of Osaka and Kobe. The company was the foremost manufacturer of seaplanes in Japan. Osaka is located on the inland sea, at the head of the long strait that separates Honshu and Shikoku islands. Arriving B-29s again assembled off the coast and started toward the city. A scene burned in my mind is that of squadron after squadron of bombers merging to form a long column above the strait. It was a serene armada, droning steadily onward among fluffy clouds.

We received a warm reception. Japanese fighters had adopted an informal tactic called Taiatari, or "body crashing." It meant ramming a bomber, sometimes head-on, sometimes catching a wing or tail. Many planes exploded after such collisions, or plunged to earth with most of their crews. We were met by one of the enemy pilots as we left the area. Fortunately, he was not as willing to die as were the Kamikaze pilots who crashed onto American warships off Okinawa. Instead he tilted his wing to catch ours as he shot by, possibly thinking he could bail out after crippling us. Captain Heath saw it coming and yanked his wing up, narrowly avoiding a crash. As we left the scene I could see a column of smoke reaching 15,000 feet into the air.

We landed on Saipan to refuel one rainy night after one of those raids. Waiting there, we saw a flash in the distance and heard an explosion.

"What was that?" someone asked.

"Looks like somebody went into the mountain. They never knew it." Eleven lives were snuffed out in that instant.

Other vignettes remain from those days. Fujiyama, the famous mountain west of Tokyo, was used as a turning point or landmark for our bomb runs. It shone mystically in the moonlight as we glided by one night on our way to Yokohama. Another image is that of bombers returning to our base on days when we had not flown. We watched from a nearby beach as dozens of aircraft arrived at dusk. They swung wide over the water and jungle in their approach patterns, landing lights on, wheels and flaps down, big birds safely home to roost. We knew the relief that their crews were feeling.

On another day in May we took part in an extremely long, solitary flight to a distant target. My recollection was that it was Sapporo, on the northernmost island of Hokkaido, but I find no record of that in the 19th Group's list of missions. Possibly it was a photography assignment. I recall looking down through broken clouds onto the rugged, snow-covered peaks below. As a lone bomber flying over remote areas, we were not worth the gas it would have taken a Japanese fighter to climb to our altitude to attack. We were in the air for well over fifteen hours.

A formation of 314th Wing B-29s on its bomb run.

We returned to the Osaka area on June 1 with 508 other B-29s on an incendiary raid. We were to be escorted over the target by Iwo Jima-based P-51 fighters after they completed their 750-mile flight to Japan. They never arrived. Unknown to us, a disaster had occurred far below as we winged our way north. Two hundred and fifty miles north of Iwo the fighters from three groups had flown straight into a severe weather front. The B-29 navigator ship leading them moved through the front without difficulty, but the small planes ran into worsening weather. The pilots became disoriented in the solid cloud cover and started colliding. Twenty-seven planes and twenty-four pilots were lost. It one was one of the little-known disasters of the war. Ten B-29s went down on the way to the target, over the target, or on the way home.

One of the most heroic individual acts of the air war occurred during one of the B-29 raids. It took place when a lead bomber from the 314th Wing was assembling a formation off the coast of Japan. The duty of the radio operator, Staff Sergeant Henry Erwin, was to drop phosphorescent smoke bombs from a launching chute beneath the plane. One of the bombs was faulty; it exploded in the chute and shot back into the bomber, striking Erwin in the face. It burned away his nose and blinded him. Realizing that the fire could destroy the airplane, he picked up the flaming bomb and groped through the smoke-filled cabin to throw the device out the pilot's window. Encountering the navigator's table in his way, he tucked the bomb under his arm, unleashed the spring lock on the table, and continued on. He threw the bomb out the window. He fell to the floor, completely aflame. Swathed in bandages at a Marianas hospital, he was awarded the Congressional Medal of Honor for his gallantry.

One of the most bizarre actions took place when the left waist blister on a B-29 blew out while the plane was 29,000 feet above Tokyo. The gunner, Sergeant James Krantz, was thrown through the open blister, where he dangled from a harness that he had made for just such an emergency. The pilot dove to a lower altitude, where it took four crewmen fifteen minutes to haul Krantz back into the bomber. He suffered severe frostbite and was battered against the side of the fuselage, but he survived.

A major weapon in the Divine Wind arsenal was the "Baka," or "Crazy Bomb," as we called it. It was a manned, rocket-powered suicide plane with a ton of explosives in its nose. It was carried aloft by a medium bomber at night and released when a B-29 was revealed by searchlights or its engine exhaust. The pilot would fall in behind the plane, then zoom ahead to smash into the tail with a devastating explosion. The Baka also was called a "ball of fire" because of the flame from its rocket. We became so apprehensive that one night we were certain we saw a Baka was flying alongside us for several minutes. It was a piercing bright light that seemed a short distance away. We watched it closely, expecting it suddenly to turn toward us. After we left the coast we realized we were looking instead at Venus.

Iwo Jima became a familiar sight as we flew to and from Japan. By the time the war ended 2,251 B-29s that were low on gas, damaged or had wounded aboard had stopped at Iwo. We landed there twice. The island was a barren, sulfurous moonscape, a bit of purgatory only three miles across at its widest and five miles long. Everything on Iwo had been flattened or scorched. The tallest structures in sight were military tents and the tails of the long line of B-29s waiting to be refueled. As we sat in the shade of a wing, two young marine privates approached us.

"You guys fly in that thing?" one asked.

"Sure," we said, acting nonchalant.

"You must be nuts."

"Why is that?"

"It's made of tin, and you can't hide. You have to sit there and take it. At least down here we can dig a hole as deep and as fast as we can go."

"We *leave* as fast as we can go," I said.

Many hours were required to gas up the bombers so Jim, Rea and I decided to walk down the slope to the beach where thousands of Marines had come ashore under heavy fire. Standing with our backs to the water, we saw Mt. Suribachi, a 546-foot extinct volcano, at our left. It dominated the beachhead. Suribachi had been heavily-defended and was taken by the Marines after four days of foot-by-foot fighting. Its capture had been memorialized by the famous photograph of six men raising the American flag at the top of the mountain.

Off to the right were the rocky caves from which Japanese soldiers had raked the beachhead. Straight ahead was an uphill climb on fine, black volcanic sand. It was a difficult return trip for us, carrying nothing. It must have been horrendous for the men who clawed their way under murderous fire, loaded with 80 to 120 pounds of equipment.

"And they think we're crazy," I said.

A total of 6,821 Marines were killed and 19,217 were wounded in taking the island over the course of five weeks. Thousands of airmen will long remember the Marines' great sacrifices.

A spectacular sight unfolded while we were waiting at Iwo one day. A crippled bomber was abandoned by its crew as it reached the island. The automatic pilot had been set, and the plane passed south over Suribachi as the airmen floated to earth. Ever so slowly, the bomber began to turn; its left wing dipped, and the plane began a long, slow, graceful arc. Faster and faster it fell, headed for an ocean area offshore that was dotted with warships and supply vessels. It seemed certain it would crash into one of them. Miraculously, it did not. The distances were deceiving; the plane hit well in front of a large cargo ship. In one instant, the wing tip was striking the water; in another, all that remained were crackling flames at the base of a tall column of black smoke. We watched in amazement.

Not long after that, we were back over Iwo on a choice assignment. Our crew was named to escort a flight of P-51s from Iwo to Japan. We would do the navigating, guide them over or around storms, then circle off-shore as they strafed targets on the ground. For that, we would get credit for a full mission. It was our reward for completing a dozen raids. Twenty-three more, and we could go home.

The single-engine fighters took off and quickly joined us. They gathered about our B-29 like chicks around a mother hen. The P-51 Mustang was among the most beautiful, and most powerful, fighter planes built in World War II. It was a shiny, sleek aircraft, with squared off wings and rudder, and a tear-drop canopy. The P-51 has been called the finest fighter produced in World War II, and the B-29 the best bomber. The two were now joined above Iwo.

The fighters were good company on the trip, for when they came near, we saw that each pilot wore a different hat over his helmet. One had on a cowboy hat, another a derby, and another a straw hat. They were a happy-go-lucky group in their swift steeds, and I envied them — even though they had to sit for several hours in their tiny cockpits.

Once we reached the coast of Japan, the fighters swept down to the attack. They were gone some time when I switched to their radio channel. As I did, one of the pilots was reporting that his plane had been hit, and that he was heading to sea to bail out. His wing man stayed close by.

"I'm getting out," the pilot said.

"Are you OK?" his buddy asked.

"Yes. They got my engine." The P-51's liquid-cooled power plant was notoriously vulnerable to ground fire.

"I'll see you back at the base," said the wing man.

I was watching the coast through clear skies. Incredibly, the two planes appeared far below, silver flies above a blue ocean. A parachute opened, and the pilot drifted down to the water. Even more astonishing, an American submarine was on duty close by to pick up downed airmen. Within sight of the homeland, the sub surfaced and plowed toward the pilot as the wing man circled above. It was something from a Hollywood film.

The rest of the fighters left the coast and started climbing toward us. They appeared as a swarm of angry bees, rather than a band of gentle chicks. Captain Heath was not sure they were our friends.

"What are they?" he asked. "What are they?" I was surprised to hear real concern in his voice.

"Doty, what are they?"

"They're '51s, captain," I said, somewhat smugly. There was no mistaking those distinctive air scoops beneath each plane. The fighters rejoined us, and we flew uneventfully back to Iwo and on to Guam.

CHAPTER NINE
Life Between Missions

We settled into a routine on Guam that spring and summer, playing boyhood games while waiting to wage war. Our days were actually quite pleasant as we teamed up in off hours for softball, made our way to a beach near the middle of the island, busied ourselves in our Quonset hut, or attended movies. Much of our time was spent in shorts and sneakers as we turned bronze under the warm sun. We strolled over to the PX tent, where we could buy Zag Nut candy bars and Fort Pitt beer. It was a terrible combination, but it was all that was available.

Jim, Ken, Hutch and I were sitting on the front porch of our hut one evening, sipping beer, when Hutch turned to me.

"Hey, Doty," he said, "how come you never learned to drink? What went wrong?"

"Nothing went wrong. Besides, I'm drinking now."

"The hell you say. You have one lousy bottle, and that's it. You've gotta learn to handle more than that."

"This one's enough," I replied.

"Didn't you drink before you came in? " Rea asked.

"No," I said. "My brother and I were working on our sister's farm over in Vermont one summer and we started going to a little church on Sunday mornings. There wasn't much else to do. We were sitting there one time when they passed a Temperance Pledge around. It was a promise never to ever drink or smoke. It sounded good, so we signed it."

"But you didn't keep the pledge."

"I kept half of it. I took it seriously and never did smoke. My father told me I shouldn't drink or smoke if I wanted to play sports. It's only when I met guys like you and Hutch that I got into trouble."

"You're not in much trouble at the rate you're going," Hutch said. "You remind me of a cheer that they used to have back at Norfolk High School. It went: 'We don't drink, and we don't smoke. Norfolk, norfolk, norfolk.' "

A crude baseball diamond was laid out not far from the flight line, where we could play between missions. One day a touring group of major league baseball players arrived for an exhibition game. Hundreds of airmen gathered along the baselines to watch "Birdie" Tebbetts, "Flash" Gordon, Enos Slaughter, "Pepper" Martin, and other major league stars. They scooped up hard grounders and whipped them across the field with smooth, fluid motions. They even staged a heated argument about a close play at home plate, throwing down their caps, swearing, spitting and kicking the dirt, treating the men to what they were missing back home.

Although we enlisted men were together with our five officers in the same bomber during our missions, we saw little of them between flights. The two groups had separate housing, mess halls, and clubs, and went their separate ways. We came together only for briefings, bombing raids, and trips to the flight line to work on our B-29 between trips to Japan.

I looked up on one of those off days to see the officers approaching en masse. Captain Heath was in the lead, his white T-shirt showing beneath a short-sleeved open blouse, his cap tipped back on his head. As they neared, I wondered if they should be called a covey of officers, or a clutch, or a pride. They seemed to move around in a band. A "braid" of officers seemed to fit best.

We enlisted men liked to joke about the system of military apartheid under which we lived, but we realized that the officers were the brains of our crew, better educated and the products of longer training. They did the flying, navigating and bombing while we simply manned the guns.

"Come on, you'all, off your duffs, " Captain Heath drawled as he entered our hut, "It's time to give the plane a bath."

We started toward the flight line on foot, picking our way around the bulldozed jungle growth. Charles Mienke and George Walker walked with the gunners, while Captain Heath and Hutch talked about engine settings and gross weights. Herb Kestenbaum joined with Paul Klenk, towering above the short bombardier.

I especially liked Mienke and Walker. On the long flights to Japan, Mienke would often find his way to the back of the plane, the only officer who did so. He would spend an hour or more sitting with us on the radar room floor. We welcomed his visits: he shared news that none of us was privy to, and he helped fill the hours. He was an impressive figure, strong physically and mentally.

Walker did not stray far from his navigator's station during the flights, but I would see him when I visited the front of the bomber on our way home. I found him to be a quiet, affable man. A slight smile often played on his lips.

"Do you think you can find our way back?" I would ask as he drew vector lines on a chart on his little desk. "Fifty-fifty right now, maybe less," he would reply. "But I'll keep working at it."

After we reached our hardstand to wash down our bomber, as our captain had ordered, the enlisted men picked up large brushes and big buckets of gasoline. We climbed onto the top of the plane through the hatch above the putt-putt and stood on a bomber back that was as broad as a whale's. Stripped down to shorts and sneakers, we washed the wings and fuselage, hoping to add two to five more miles an hour of speed. We mounted ladders to polish our windows until they gleamed, the better to see enemy fighters.

Someone — the reports blamed stateside religious groups, Eleanor Roosevelt or an offended general — had objected to the racy art and names that had been given to the B-29s. The order came down that "Dauntless Dotty," "Party Girl," "Stripped for Action," "Heavenly Body," and the other voluptuous women would have to be replaced by less offensive artwork. Our group decided on names that could not be more arcane: the home towns of crew members. We drew straws, Jim Dudley won, and our B-29 became "The City of College Park."

"That name really is inspiring," I told Dudley. "I'm all fired up."

"It could be a lot worse than that," he said. "Suppose it was 'The Hamlet of Hudson Falls?' Ah don't believe I'd want to even get into a plane with that name."

We also could have our own names painted beneath our positions on the plane. In a romantic moment I had them print "Andy and Bake" beneath my window.

Jim and Rea won a different drawing. The three of us had become sergeants before we went overseas, and the time came when two of us could be promoted to staff sergeant. I drew the short straw, and remained a buck sergeant at less pay. It was a cruel choice to be made by men who shared the same duties, but there was no court of appeals.

A movie played every night at the crude outdoor theater. The seats were empty ammunition boxes. Everyone carried a flashlight, a poncho and a helmet liner, for it rained nearly every evening. Waiting in the drizzle for the film to begin, the men played games with their flashlight beams, darting them wildly across the dark screen. Sometimes a large insect would fly over. Several flashlights would fasten onto it and follow relentlessly. I wondered if the bug felt as uncomfortable as we had under similar circumstances over Tokyo.

One movie in particular remains fresh in my mind. It featured Gloria DeHaven. She wore a sheer, low-cut satin gown that hugged her hips. As she sang "I've Got You Under My Skin," her hands caressed her thighs. One could almost hear the rustle of virile young men being aroused throughout the area.

We improved our living quarters. Quonset huts were made of sheets of corrugated steel curved over large metal arches. There were no interior supporting posts; small windows were placed at points in the sides of the building. Only screens were needed at the recessed ends of the huts.

Our structure housed only the enlisted men of two crews, which gave us room to spread out with single bunks. I scrounged up some wood from bomb crates, borrowed a hammer and saw, and made a desk. It sat next to my bunk. There I carved a wooden camel and named him Cosmo because I liked the alliteration of Cosmo the Camel. I sent him to Bake, and he rests on a shelf at home today.

Seated at the desk, I corresponded often with relatives, high school friends, and of course with Bake. She and I wrote virtually every day. Most of my creative energy went into a stream of letters home and to friends in the service. None of the letters have survived. In fact, few of my reports about our combat experiences got beyond Guam; the recipients wrote that my letters often arrived with entire paragraphs scissored out by officers in our group, who censored the mail of enlisted men. Although the officers' mail was said to be censored, as well, I have since read books based largely on letters sent home by pilots, navigators and bombardiers, complete with details about the missions flown, losses suffered, and damage caused — the same, or more, information that had been excised from our pages.

For a time I recorded each of our bombing missions on one of the tagged pins that were removed by our bombardier to activate our bombs before they were dropped. Rea picked one up from my desk and read it.

"Kanoya airfield — April 26. Moderate flak," he read. "How cute." I was embarrassed, and later threw the pins away. What valuable mementos they would be now, fifty years later.

Bake's letters came in batches, two or three at a time. She reported on what was happening back home: who was entering service, who was home on leave, who had been wounded or killed, and what was going on at the Iron and Brass works. With the town emptied of young men her age, she spent most of her time with her friends, Claire Carleton and Rosemary Fant. Her letters did not speak of deep love or of a future together. We had known each other a short time, and were still young. But she would confess: "I miss our blue chair," where she had sat on my lap late at night in her house as the soft music played. She told me after the war that she was certain I would return, for I had not expressed fear about what we had to do.

We received the welcome news that Germany had surrendered on May 2, 1945. I was pleased to think that hundreds of additional aircraft and warships, and dozens of new infantry divisions, would soon be making their way to the Pacific theater. Not long after that, a letter from my brother Bill arrived reporting that my twin was missing in action. I was hit hard by the news, for I had failed to respond to Chuck's suggestion, before he went overseas, that I should help him transfer into the Air Force. Out of guilt, I'm sure, I vowed that I would somehow make my way to Europe after the war to visit his grave if he were dead. Even so, I felt strangely confident that he would be found. He was strong, self-sufficient, and adventurous. No doubt he had simply been separated from his unit during the confusing last days of the war. A week later, another letter arrived to report that he was safe; he and a few others had ranged far ahead to look at the equipment of the Soviet soldiers who had moved in from the East.

"We're going to have to fight those guys sooner or later," Chuck wrote. "I just wanted to see what kind of equipment they had." I could imagine him befriending Soviet troops and walking among them, a cigarette dangling from his lips. As he did, he would carefully look over their rifles, machine guns and vehicles.

Members of our gang from Hudson Falls devised ways to let others know their whereabouts, despite military censorship. I wrote to my friends to tell them I had heard that "Kobe" was stationed on Guam. That was the nickname they had given me in high school after I had mimicked the way Japanese fighter pilots in goggles and fur-lined helmets in the movies had gleefully pointed down at targets to be attacked.

A similar exchange told me that Chuck Eagle was stationed on Okinawa with an Army artillery unit. I composed a letter, ostensibly from Chuck, about a basketball game that his unit had played against a group of natives after the island had been secured. I signed his name to it, and sent it to the sports editor of the Glens Falls *Post Star*. It was sheer fabrication, but the editor printed it verbatim.

According to the story, the men in Chuck's unit had built a basketball court in their spare time. The local natives, "when not toiling in the rice paddies," appeared at courtside, "barefoot and clad in loin cloths." They quickly caught onto the game, and asked to try their hand at set shots and lay-ups. They were led by a sharp-shooter named Kobe. The Okinawans soon improved enough to challenge the Americans to a game. Chuck's unit accepted. I described the mythical contest that took place before hundreds of cheering soldiers, sailors and marines, how well Chuck had played, and mailed the letter.

Later on, I learned that I had been tricked: the squadron officers who censored my unsealed letters saw that I had also written to Bake. In what must have been a delicious moment, they switched the messages. Bake's letter went to the editor, and his to her. She ultimately delivered the game letter to him, and retrieved her own.

Reality crept in when we did not expect it. Playing softball one afternoon, we looked up to see smoke billowing over the runway. We ran over to find a bomber in flames after it had careened off the landing strip. The plane was surrounded by men and equipment who were pouring foam onto the fire to rescue those inside. They carefully removed a badly-burned crewman from the wreckage. The tail gunner and a few others in the back of the plane survived.

Another time we were trucked to Harmon Field in the middle of the island, where a B-29 had landed the day before with a mortally wounded crewman aboard. We were to return the bomber to North Field. The man was the central fire control gunner. The only damage to the aircraft was a nickel-sized hole in the plastic dome above his position. A bit of steel had pierced the dome and his flak helmet, taking his life. Most of the blood on the seat and the floor had been scrubbed away, but traces of it remained. Abe Veroba did not ride in the CFC position on the short hop back home.

Late that spring, a fifth wing — the 315th — began arriving at a new base on the northwest side of Guam. We welcomed the help from its four bombardment groups and twelve fresh squadrons, but I was aware of an attitude that may exist among all fighting men. I looked upon the new crews as late-comers who had missed our tougher earlier missions. In the very same way, the original members of our group no doubt saw our replacement crew in the same light — much as the older '29 units on Saipan and Tinian must have viewed our 314th Wing on Guam — and as the 58th Wing pioneers from crude bases in China and India surely regarded the Marianas airmen. And so it goes: Eighth and Fifteenth Air Force veterans of the hellish missions over Germany in 1943 and 1944 probably perceived their successors — and the 20th Air Force in its fancy B-29s — as men who had no idea of how terrible aerial warfare can really be.

Something else happens, as well. Although it is seldom mentioned, those who come under serious, sustained enemy fire feel superior to those in support positions who do not face danger. The mechanics, cooks, ordinance men, truck drivers, weather officers and others were absolutely vital and shared the hardships of military duty far from home, but they were safe, and virtually certain to survive the war. That helps explain why there is little sympathy among many World War II veterans for a national president who avoided serving in his generation's conflict in Vietnam — even in a support capacity — no matter how valid his reasons. They responded when the nation called, and he did not.

There was no escaping the base public address system, which covered every area of our encampment. Our peaceful interlude between missions suddenly would end when we heard the loud click that preceded an announcement. We would stop whatever we were doing, look up at the speakers, and listen. It was time to get serious again.

"The following crews are alerted for briefing at 1300 hours: Crew number two, Captain Lawless. Crew number three, Captain Munger. Crew number five, Captain Handwerker." We would wait as our number neared. "Crew number eleven, Captain Heath."

Our first thought was: where were we going? The Tokyo-Nagoya area was dreaded. Missions to other Japanese cities and targets were easier. The moment we entered the briefing tent, our eyes went to the map. If the red line slanted left to a lesser city or Shikoku or Kyushu islands, we were relieved, and joked a little more among ourselves; if it pointed north to Honshu, we said nothing.

We went down to our plane before briefing to help refuel and arm it. A small tractor pulled a train of 250, 500, or 1000-pound bombs into place beneath the plane. The ordinance men hoisted the bombs into place in the bays with winches to attach them to the bomb racks. The gunners stretched long belts of ammunition on the ground — 1200 rounds per gun — to check for defects. I stowed my belts in the metal boxes near the tail. It was hot work in the narrow area to layer the belts into the boxes and feed them into the tracks of rollers that led into the tail turret.

After completing that task, I went to the rear of the airplane to climb a tall stand behind the tail turret. I removed the turret covers, lifted the lids of the two guns, and pulled the cartridges along the roller chutes and into the weapons. I loaded the guns "hot," actuating them with a screwdriver to slam the rounds into the firing chamber. It was at this time that the armorer helping me would disappear. The first round could go off prematurely in the face of the gunner as it went home, so my helper would find other things to do at that moment.

"Where are you going?" I would ask innocently. He continued on his way. "Miserable coward," I thought to myself. He was safe on the ground throughout the war, yet could not take a simple risk. It made me feel good to grumble to myself about his timidity.

Once the bomber was ready, hours before take-off, I wondered what lay ahead. Many times I watched the sun set, and speculated where I would be when the sun went down the next day. Safely back at the base? In a Japanese prison camp? Wounded or dead? Adrift in the ocean? Was there a bullet or a bit of steel resting somewhere in Japan at that moment that was destined to tear into my body the next day? If our plane were hit and spinning to earth, would I be able to fight my way out the escape window in time? What would happen if we had to bail out and were captured?

"Do you know what the British did to the Germans that they shot down during the Blitz?" Rea asked us one night in our hut. "They strung them up in a hurry."

Good Lord, I thought, if the phlegmatic English could do that, what could we expect from the frenzied Japanese? "Tokyo Rose," the English-speaking Japanese announcer who taunted Americans with radio messages, warned us that B-29 crewmen would be hanged as war criminals if captured because of what they had done to helpless civilians. We learned after the war that outraged Japanese had beheaded some downed crewmen, and had even kicked and beaten the bodies of those who had crashed. Our greatest hope, we were told, was to be taken prisoner by policemen or soldiers in an outlying area.

In my bunk at night, I ran through a fantasy: if we were shot down I would bail out, land in a wooded area, and bury my parachute. Hiding in the trees, I would wait for darkness, then slowly make my way to a fishing village on the coast. At the village I would steal a boat and paddle out to sea, where I would be spotted by a friendly airplane or submarine. I did not bother myself with the realities of distance, hunger, my Caucasian appearance, or alert Japanese dogs. It was sheer self-delusion, of course, but it was better than thinking about other fates.

My sister Ruth had given me a small Bible when I left home. Although ours was not a religious family, I kept the Bible over my heart on every mission. I also recited the Lord's Prayer the same way each time, being sure to thank God in a P. S. at the end. It seemed to bring me good luck, so I never deviated from the routine.

My head told me that it was highly unlikely that a superior force somewhere in the universe could be protecting me, other crews, enemy pilots and Japanese civilians all at the same time, but my heart told me cling to some form of divine intervention. There was no harm done in believing, and possibly some good.

Daylight missions called for us to be aroused in the middle of the night, shortly after we had been able to drop off to sleep. We splashed water in our faces and made our way in the darkness to the brightly-lighted mess hall. The halls were built to a standard design; an entry aisle down one side, serving tables across the front, and heavy tables aligned throughout the room. Still drowsy and blinking in the bright light, we lined up as scrambled eggs, bacon and toast were placed on our metal trays. We ate quietly and drank our coffee.

If we were to hit Japan at midnight, we left late in the afternoon to be over the target several hours later. We would sit in the shade of our bomber until it was time to pull the propellers through and take our positions. Now a seasoned crew, we bantered as we waited.

"I heard a great story today," Lieutenant Walker said. "I don't know if it's true or not, but the way it goes, a B-29 from Saipan was returning from a mission when the AC spotted an aircraft carrier up ahead and decided to have some fun. So he feathered one engine, lowered the landing gear, and dropped down as if he was in trouble and going to land. By the time the plane was half a mile away, everybody on the carrier was out on the deck, blinking lights and waving him off with everything from shirts to flags to the captain's hat. The pilot pulled up the wheels and flaps, gunned the engines, and zoomed away. The Navy guys were fit to be tied."

We all laughed, picturing the pandemonium aboard the carrier.

"That's a good one," Klenk said. "I wonder if it really happened."

"Of course not," Heath said. "Somebody would get their ass court-martialed fast for a trick like that."

"But you have to admit it would be fun," Mienke said.

"You'all can bet the Navy wouldn't put up with that kind of stunt for a minute," Heath added. "Every gun aboard ship would open up. They can't take any chances, any more than we can." Prophetic words.

The talk turned to life after the war. Jim Dudley told us that he wanted to go home, get married, and play professional baseball. He had come from a large high school and was a good athlete. If he failed to make a semipro team, he would study to become a pharmacist. His girl friend was waiting for him back in Georgia.

"She's a real Georgia peach," he said. "Ah believe she's the prettiest woman I ever laid my eyes on." Her picture was perched near his bunk in our hut. Jim would pick it up and kiss it now and then. "What a peach," he would repeat. "I wish I was with her now."

Rea Schuessler was anxious to return to his job at the University of Alabama. He loved the Crimson Tide football team and all it stood for. Rea could recite past game scores and statistics at length, and deplored the fact that a world war had gotten in the way of his school's powerful football program.

Hutch told us little about his past in New Jersey. He was something of an enigma to me. He was rough-hewn, but good-natured. Intelligent enough to understand the workings of complex machinery, he nevertheless seemed uninterested in matters not having to do with the care and feeding of Wright R-3350 engines. Hutch was a bit out of shape, his tummy rounding out above the top of his trousers. I felt that he was amused by the innocent activities of the younger gunners, and liked to tease us about it. He was almost like an older brother.

No one expressed fear as we waited. It was not the manly thing to do, and it could reduce overall crew effectiveness. We kept it all inside. We talked about the coming target, about our duties, and about the tons of incendiary bombs we were about to drop on some Japanese city, but never about death or wounds. Rea's comment about our fate should we be captured was the only one of its kind that I remember.

"Do you ever wonder what happens down there when all those bombs hit?" Abe asked one day.

"Not a bit," Mienke said. "I don't think about it at all, and I don't feel a bit sorry. Look what they did to China and Pearl Harbor, and to the people they capture. They're a ruthless bunch of bastards when they get the upper hand. They don't show any mercy, and they don't deserve any. It's that simple." We nodded in agreement. "One of the last truly innocent generations of Americans" had become tolerant of brutality. That may have been the greatest change in me during my two years of military service.

As we waited, I examined the light survival vest that I wore over my flight suit to be sure the pockets held a mirror, shark repellent, fishline and fishhooks, first aid items, a tube of morphine, and other materials.

I learned our emergency procedures well, especially those that dealt with parachuting out at high altitude, or into the sea. The emergency bail-out bottle of oxygen would be needed if I opened my chute five miles above the earth, where the air was thin. If I leaped without a bottle, I would delay pulling my rip-cord until I had dropped down to where I could breathe without trouble. I paid particular attention to the way I would attach my life raft to my parachute harness and how I would unfasten my parachute straps before inflating my Mae West as I drifted down to the ocean.

I carried a length of parachute cord with me on every mission to use as a tourniquet in case I needed it. When I got back into my tail compartment I would hang the cord around the base of my gun sight where it would be handy if I were wounded in an arm or leg.

Despite all my precautions, I made a shocking discovery one night as we were taxiing out to take off. Parachute harnesses generally incorporated two strong chest snaps that hooked onto the two "O"- shaped fixtures on the chest chute itself. Sometimes the fittings would be reversed, with the "O"s on the harness and the snaps on the chute. Standing by the putt-putt as we moved out, I noticed that all four of my fixtures were "O"s, which meant it would not be possible to fasten them together. I, or the parachute outfitters, had become complacent. I quickly reported the news.

"Tail to Captain. I've got a problem. I've got the wrong parachute."

"Dammit!" he said. "Go find one, fast."

I dropped out the rear door and ran toward some buildings, determined to break into a supply room if I had to. I found one that was open and threw my useless chute to a surprised clerk. He gave me the proper one and I raced to catch our plane as it inched forward in a line of bombers. I tossed the chute inside and hauled myself into the rear door, exhausted by the effort. We took off as scheduled. I shuddered to think of what might have happened had I not discovered the problem and we had been forced to abandon our plane that day. I have since stood beneath a B-29, looking up at that door, and am amazed to think I once pulled myself into it unaided. There is nothing like a good shot of adrenaline.

The stress of the take-offs cannot be overemphasized. The pilot needed full power as long as he could have it to haul his overloaded bomber into the air. The B-29 was designed to carry a gross weight of 120,000 pounds and a maximum of 135,000 pounds, but they often weighed in at more than 140,000 pounds. The rule of thumb was that a bomber needed to gain a mile an hour of take-off speed for every thousand pounds of weight. Thus a B-29 weighing 120,000 pounds would have to accelerate to 120 miles an hour, and a 141,000-pound airplane to 141 miles an hour before lifting off the ground.

The flight engineer, knowing that the engines could quickly overheat at top speed, especially on a hot day, preferred the engine cowls to be open as far as possible for cooling during the take-off. But wide-open cowls reduced the speed of the plane, so subtle compromises had to be reached. The engineer also wanted the pilot to throttle back an engine that was running too hot, but the pilot demanded every ounce of power he could get. If an engine failed after the "point of no return" was reached, tragedy could result. Among the saddest sights to be seen by departing crews as they took off was the flaming wreckage of a bomber below them at the end of the runway. (When the B-29 Enola Gay took off from Tinian a few months later to drop an atomic bomb on Hiroshima, the bombardier refused to arm the device before the aircraft was airborne because B-29s "regularly crashed on take-off." He said he did not want to wipe Tinian off the map.)

Nature and machinery were major enemies. The weather fronts on the way to Japan and over the home islands, the vast distances, the capricious engines, all took their toll. Dozens of bombers had to turn back from every large-scale mission because of mechanical problems. So many planes fell into the sea en route to Japan or on their return that an elaborate air-sea rescue system involving airplanes, ships and submarines had to be created. By war's end, fourteen submarines, twenty-one Navy seaplanes, nine "Superdumbos" (B-29s carrying a lifeboat and equipment to be dropped into the sea) and five ships were on station, ready to come to the aid of downed airmen.

Once we were on our way to Japan, we spent our time watching the engines, talking about the war and when it might end, napping on the radar room floor, or listening to radio broadcasts from San Francisco.

"This is Master Sergeant Melvin Cohen of the Armed Forces Radio Network in San Francisco, bringing you the news of the day," the professional voice proclaimed as we flew northward. "First, the headlines: In Europe, American troops are pressing on toward

Berlin, and are nearing Leipzig, Austria. The British Army is twenty-five miles from Hamburg. In the Pacific, the island of Okinawa has been secured by the Army and Marines. Also in the Pacific theater, our B-29s have destroyed Japanese Kamikaze bases on the island of Kyushu."

"That's us," Ken Cox broke in.

"Who said they were destroyed?" Dudley asked. "Ah believe they were still there last I saw."

The announcer continued with the news, concluding with the events on the home front. The nation was returning to normal under President Truman, and the war was being supported wholeheartedly. Rosie the Riveter and Mike the Machinist were feverishly turning out planes and guns and ships and were collecting war bonds like stamps every pay day. The announcer concluded by wishing us all a pleasant good afternoon.

"Thanks a lot, Melvin."

"Rough duty," a crewman said. "San Francisco in wartime."

"And a goddamn master sergeant at that."

"Lucky son of a bitch. All those women to himself. Now he'll go out on the town."

"And get laid."

"Again."

I pondered the meaning of those statements as we flew on.

On one of his visits to the rear of the plane, Lieutenant Mienke spoke of the coming invasion of the Japan home islands by American soldiers and marines.

"It's coming sure as hell, and it's not going to be easy," he said. "I wouldn't be at all surprised if there were some landings this fall, and it's going to be a real bitch. The Japanese will throw everything they have at us."

He talked in a general way about wartime losses.

"You know, there are acceptable losses in a war, and unacceptable losses. If only a few percent of us go down on a mission, LeMay can live with that with no trouble. But if fifteen to twenty per cent of us get knocked off consistently, that's real trouble. That means we're losing planes and crews faster than they can be replaced. We couldn't keep that up very long."

"Especially if the we is us," I said.

Life Between Missions 117

19th Bombardment Group B-29s en route to Japan.

Bombers from the author's squadron pass by Fujiyama on their way to a target.

"That's true. But the war will go on. That's what wars are all about. Keep pushing until something gives, as long as you can afford it."

Acceptable losses, I thought. What a good name for a book.

Hundreds of miles from Japan, we returned to our positions. I crawled back into the tail to set up shop in my small domain. I put on my light helmet with its small intercom receivers in the ears and inserted the line into the jack box. Next came a throat microphone, held by a black elastic band that I snapped around my neck. I put on my hard rubber oxygen mask, fastened it to my helmet and plugged the long hose into the ship's system.

A multi-pocketed survival vest fitted over my flight suit, and my parachute harness went over that. I fastened my harness leg and chest straps, and clicked the chest chute in place. Next came a flak vest, an apron made up of small, overlapping plates of tough steel, much like a coat of medieval armor. The final touch was a heavy metal flak helmet. I switched on my gun sight and turret.

"Tail in position and ready," I reported.

"Roger," came the reply.

I had a sweeping view in three directions, some protection provided by the shielding and the flak vest and helmet, and an escape hatch so close by that I could actually tumble out of it when opened. By folding my seat back and sliding it up as we approached the coast, I gained more room. That also would make it easier for the other gunners to reach me in my compartment should I be wounded.

Standing by my gun sight, I was as calm and confident as one can be under those circumstances. I flattered myself that I had been entrusted with the defense of a million-dollar bomber and her crew. I was Horatius, the Roman soldier I had admired in high school, ready to hold off the Visigoths.

After we left behind the target and the coast we began shedding our equipment. I generally remained in the tail for another hour or so to keep watch and wait until we reached a lower altitude. Then I could pass through the unpressurized area to the waist cabin without an oxygen mask.

Some of my most pleasant memories of the war have to do with the hours spent with the other gunners in the waist, returning home after a mission. Even the airplane seemed lighter and happier, engines purring, as we descended slowly to a lower level. The afternoon sun streamed into the ship as we listened to music, ate a packed lunch (with the inevitable canned fruit cocktail), and unwound. I can still hear Charley Barnett's "Pompton Turnpike" in my headset as we cruised home.

Sometimes I would crawl through the tunnel into the front cabin, pushing my parachute ahead of me. I did not trust the engines enough to leave it far behind, even after many missions. Ken Cox sat wearing his headphones by his radio, George Walker plotted our way home, and Hutch's eyes kept roaming the dials that virtually surrounded him. Hutch reached out to punch my shoulder as I passed by.

"How ya doing, gunner?" he would ask.

"Great. How are you? Better yet, how are the engines doing?"

"Looking good. No problems."

I often made my way to the bombardier's seat in the glass nose of the plane, where I sat enthralled as we soared home between towering cumulus clouds. Other times, I knelt in the padded tunnel between the front and waist compartments to look out the small plastic dome from which George Walker took his navigational sightings. From there I watched engines that droned on steadily for hour after hour, and marveled at man's ability to create machinery of that kind.

If we were returning at night we took turns keeping an eye on the engines from the waist as others slept. It was hard staying awake through the long dark hours. We were told that there were times when apparently everyone aboard a B-29 fell asleep and the plane slipped down into the ocean without their knowing it.

The landings found me back in the tail position, for I had noticed that the tail of an airplane often was all that remained intact after a crash. We entered our landing pattern, then slowed perceptively as the wheels were lowered and the flaps slid down from the rear edge of the wings. The big flaps looked like huge, drooping elephant ears.

"Left flap and wheels fully down," Rea called out. Jim added his report. We slowed, banked over the jungle, dropped down, and skimmed in for a landing. The wheels screeched as they touched, sending up puffs of smoke. The twin nose wheels followed as we breathed a sigh of relief.

Once on the ground, I opened the escape window to let in the warm air. Leaning on the sill, the tail gently rising and falling, I watched as we passed parked bombers, fuel trucks, jeeps and tents. We entered our hardstand, pivoted, and shut down the engines. We were pleased and tired, another mission behind us.

As we taxied in one night a silver identification bracelet that I wore on my left wrist came loose and fell onto the pavement. We were far from our revetment, so I did not go out the next day to look for the bracelet. Bombers following us may well have pressed it flat into the asphalt. Perhaps that bracelet, embedded in the pavement and bearing my name and serial number, will be unearthed by archaeologists thousands of years from now, much as today's scholars have found the personal items of Roman soldiers who served along ancient walls in England. We all crave some form of immortality.

Sometimes war correspondents would be waiting to talk to the early arrivals. They always seemed to be hurried, sweaty and unshaven in their green, rumpled uniforms.

A truck would take us back for debriefing. Afterward, we were given a shot of whiskey. I didn't care for mine, but Hutch was always willing to take it off my hands. Then it was back to the hut to wash up and go to bed. If the timing was right, we could catch a shower in a newly-rigged system. A few days to a week later, we would repeat a journey that took far longer than does a commercial jet trip from San Francisco to London today. But we knew that we enjoyed comforts between those trips that combat infantrymen and marines could only dream about.

Chapter Ten
"They're Running Out of Gas"

Japan was taking a fearful pounding that spring and summer. The 20th Air Force had been built up to the point where it could send out nine hundred bombers at a time. Thirteen thousand tons of bombs fell on Japan in March, 42,000 tons in July, and 100,000 tons a month at war's end. The major cities were destroyed in fire raids, so the B-29s turned their attention to the lesser communities. On many nights, as many as 720 bombers (four wings) left their bases in the Marianas for simultaneous incendiary attacks on four different cities, one wing per city. Sixty-five Japanese cities went up in flames before the war came to an end.

As I look today upon pictures of graceful Japanese homes and the simple elegance of their hand-crafted furniture, I can only speculate on the thousands of antique treasures that must have helped to fuel those terrible fires.

With the war over in Europe, a growing force of American power was shifted to the Pacific to join the B-29 campaign. The '29s, A-26s, P-51s, Okinawa-based B-24s and Navy carrier planes were roaming over Japan, almost with impunity, shooting at virtually anything that moved.

The *New York Times* editorialized: "They asked for it. They are getting it."

We felt no remorse, remembering the sneak attack on Pearl Harbor and Japanese soldiers' brutal treatment of the people they conquered. And unlike fighting men on the ground, we were far removed from the suffering we caused far below. We engaged in anonymous destruction. There is a serene isolation in aerial warfare, except when antiaircraft fire explodes on all sides or a fighter bores in.

The practice of bombing open cities began in 1849, when an Austrian hot air balloon was used to drop small explosive devices on the city of Venice. In 1914, a German Taube monoplane dropped five small bombs near a Paris railroad station to usher in the age of aerial bombardment. As World War I progressed, German zeppelins bombed London indiscriminately, and British bombers retaliated against German cities.

Between the two world wars, efforts were made to ban aerial attacks on civilian populations, but the proposals were rejected after military officers pointed out that legitimate targets might be located within cities and should not be exempted. The military also realized that widespread bombing of cities could be a way to demoralize an enemy and hasten his surrender in future wars.

Thus World War II opened with the Luftwaffe's wanton bombing of Warsaw and Rotterdam to speed the downfall of those cities. The London blitz soon followed, as did British reprisals against German cities. After that, cities became fair game; both Allied and Axis air forces routinely dropped tons of demolition and incendiary bombs on the homes, schools, churches, businesses and hospitals of their enemies. Most of the destruction that took place in World War II was random.

I wrote home to my parents before our fifteenth mission. "This should all be over pretty soon," I said. "The Japs can't keep it up. They're running out of gas."

We took off for Osaka early in the morning of June 7. Herb Kestenbaum was ill, and was replaced by a young radar officer, Richard O'Brien. He was quiet on our flight north, a handsome fellow among strangers, intent on the green radar screen in his dark room.

We were fairly confident it would be an easy run, for we had seen few fighters in recent weeks and the antiaircraft fire was growing weaker. The flight was even easier than we expected; all of Japan was blanketed by heavy clouds. We saw no land from the time we neared the coast until we left it. We bombed by radar and saw only a few bursts of flak well away from our bomber.

A hundred miles off the coast on our way home, we began to relax. I was still watching behind us when something caught my eye. Far to the rear, to my lower right, a twin-engine fighter plane popped up above the clouds, then dropped down. He was on the prowl, hoping to catch us by surprise.

"Tail to crew," I called out. "A fighter just came out of the clouds at seven o'clock low and dropped back down. Get ready."

It was an Irving, the name that had been given to a night fighter that was equipped with radar and heavy armament. I entered his wingspan into my gun sight and waited. The black plane suddenly emerged a few thousand yards to the rear, climbing rapidly at my lower left.

"Five o'clock low," I cried out, and found him in my sight. I narrowed the circle of dots down to his wing tips, and began squeezing off bursts. He opened fire at the same time. The machine guns in his wings flared again and again as he closed in. His glowing tracer bullets flew lazily by, looking almost harmless. He kept coming until he was a few hundred yards away. The image of that black fighter, his winking guns and the slow-motion tracers will stay with me forever.

I slowly opened the ring to hold it around his wing tips, and continued firing. I was aware that I was spacing my bursts, letting up for a few seconds as he bore in. My bullets were striking his right engine, sending parts flying. Smoke began pouring from the engine, and the pilot broke off his attack. He banked down into the clouds, a long, black plume trailing behind. I have often wondered if he made it home safely, and where he is today. One of his engines was still operating, so he probably was able to return to his base.

Late that day, as we were nearing home, I was spelling Rea in his waist position when I became aware that something was wrong. Captain Heath and Hutch were talking about headwinds and the amount of fuel that remained in our wing tanks, as they so often did. But this time I could tell they were worried. Finally Hutch said, "It's going to be close."

Not long after, Captain Heath came onto the intercom.

"We've got a little problem up here," he said. "We've hit some headwinds, and might not be able to make it back. Y'all should get ready, in case we have to ditch or bail out."

By that time, we were well south of Saipan and forty-five miles north of Guam. So not only the Japanese were running out of gas. I scrambled quickly back to the tail, where my life raft rested in its canvas pack within the seat frame. I snapped my chest parachute onto my harness. (Thank God the fixtures matched.) Listening from the tail, I could hear that the situation was worsening.

I lifted out the life raft pack and attached it to the rings on the bottom of my parachute harness. A long strap hung from the raft inside the pack. I pulled the strap underneath my harness and snapped it onto my Mae West. It was an ingenious arrangement; once I shucked the 'chute harness in the water and yanked on the strap, the raft would be pulled free of the pack and automatically inflate.

I folded my seat back and slid it up to give myself more room. The intercom clicked.

"No time left," Captain Heath said. "Everybody out." A frightened voice broke in. It was the replacement radar officer. "I can't swim," he cried out. "I can't swim."

"You don't have to," I said. "Just remember your procedures." The life vest and raft should be enough.

The bail-out bell began ringing. I unplugged my headset, unsnapped my throat microphone, and opened the escape window. The air whipped by in a fearsome roar. As I moved to dive out, I found I could not; I was caught by the life raft strap, which had become snagged in the folded seat. I felt a wave of panic, and began tugging desperately at the strap. It would not come loose. The bell kept ringing. I thought of cutting the strap with my knife, but told myself to calm down to work the strap free. I unfolded the seat, slid it back down, and released the strap. I pushed the seat up, and went out the window.

First there was a rush and roar of air, then I tumbled over and over. Suddenly the parachute opened above me with a "pop" and I was jerked to a halt. I have no memory of pulling the ripcord handle, or where it went afterward. My helmet was gone. It was strangely quiet except for the hum of our disappearing bomber. The evening sky was still pink from the sunset as I floated down.

I could see another chute against the black sea below, and called out to its owner. I undid my chest and leg straps and inflated my Mae West so that I could get out of the harness as quickly as possible after landing. I dangled there like a kid on a swing. As I watched, the horizon quickly closed in. For the first time, I realized that I would be alone in the ocean. I landed with a hard splash on my back and sank far deeper into the water than I ever imagined. It seemed a long time before I came up to the surface, even with an inflated vest. But I kept my mouth closed and held my breath until I surfaced. I threw off the parachute harness and pulled the life raft strap. The raft came out of its pack, and a gas cylinder opened it with a "whoosh." I drew the small raft to me and climbed in.

The waves were rolling monsters, flecks of white spray whipping from their crests. I rode them up and down as if on a roller coaster. Even when I was carried high on a wave, I saw no other crew members. I spent the night trying to sleep, being tipped over by the big swells, climbing back into the raft, and drying off — only to be tipped over again. I was glad I had not cut the strap, for it kept the raft from blowing away when I was spilled into the water. Each time I was dumped into the sea, I thought about the possibility of sharks being in the area and scrambled back into the raft as quickly as I could.

A squall moved in. I collected rain in the rubber raft cover, washed the salt away as best I could, and drank all I could hold. I did not know how long it would be until help arrived.

Just before dawn, I noticed a dark shape in the distance. For a time I thought it was Rota, a small, Japanese-held island just north of Guam that had been by-passed. I did not want to be washed ashore, for B-29s that had to abort their missions dumped their bombs there before returning to Guam. The soldiers were not likely to be kind. I reversed the yellow side of the cover to the dark blue side and snuggled down even lower in the raft.

After a time, I heard the muffled chugging of an engine. The dark shape was a merchant ship that was looking for us. A searchlight swept the ocean. "Ship ahoy," I called out, as they did in the movies. The beam came my way, and I waved my arms. It lighted on me. Soon the side of the ship loomed high above. A sailor came down a cargo net, grabbed my hand, and helped me out of the raft. I scrambled up the side, only to find my legs weak when I climbed over the railing and stood on the deck. Members of the ship's crew stood watching the strange scene. I was led below, given a hot shower, a shot of whiskey, an officer's underwear and bunk, and fell asleep.

Rea and Jim were picked up before I was. Rea said later that someone told him that another member of the crew had been found, and that "he came up the side of the ship like a monkey."

"That must be our tail gunner," Rea said.

Three other members of the crew were not as fortunate. George Walker and Donald Hutchison failed to open their life rafts and had drowned. They were found floating in their life vests, unable to keep their heads out of the choppy waves all night. Ken Cox was able to do that; he did not get his raft open, but he fought to keep his head up. His neck was scraped raw by his life vest, but he survived.

I assumed that Lieutenant O'Brien, the replacement radar man who could not swim, had leaped from the plane after I did. In the most bizarre aspect of the entire tragedy, I did not learn otherwise for many years. In actuality, O'Brien had gone down with the plane, refusing to jump despite the pleas of Rea, Jim and Abe. They considered throwing him out the rear door, but Abe thought he could persuade him to jump by himself. Abe argued as long as he could, then had to leap before it was too late. The radar man preferred to die in a crash rather than risk drowning in the sea.

Jim, Rea and Abe never talked about those awful moments, nor did I ever ask about them. Their need to deny or forget was complete, and I must have undergone the same subconscious process. It was only after I was reunited with Jim Dudley forty-five years after the war that I learned the true story.

We could only speculate on what had happened to George and Hutch. Possibly they had left their rafts behind. Possibly they had forgotten to attach the raft straps to their life vests, or had attached their straps over their chute harnesses instead of underneath them. Nor did we ever find out why we had not stopped at Iwo, Tinian or Saipan to refuel. There was an unspoken agreement that the enlisted men should not press Captain Heath too much on the subject, so we did not. We knew our place, and stuck to it.

My impression was that Captain Heath disliked the long fueling delays, and enjoyed the attention that early arrivals from a mission received. He may have been eager to get back to report that we had beaten off an enemy fighter at a time when few were left in the skies. Whatever the reason, three young men paid with their lives.

Our encounter with the Irving was never reported; the damage inflicted on a Japanese fighter was incidental in light of what had happened to our bomber and the three men. I have since wondered if other B-29s that mysteriously disappeared off the coast of Japan without a trace during the war had fallen victim to surprise attacks such as ours.

A few days later we gathered at a military cemetery outside of Agana. The burial ground was located on a hillside, overlooking the Pacific. The sun was shining, a light breeze was blowing, and clouds were piled high in the sky. It was a glorious summer day. Our lives were continuing on; three others had come to an end.

An olive-drab Army ambulance with a large red cross arrived, bearing the remains of George Walker and Donald Hutchison in wooden coffins with rope handles. I wondered where O'Brien's body was. Thinking that he also had drowned, I assumed he was to be buried by members of his own crew at another time.

We opened the rear doors of the ambulance and slid Hutch's coffin toward us. As we did, the box tilted, and blood trickled from a crack onto the ground. The officers bore George to his open grave as we carried Hutch to his. The graves were located side by side, approximating the way the two men had sat across an aisle from each other for hundreds of hours in the air. After an Air Force chaplain performed the funeral service Abe Veroba stepped up to the graves and wailed a Hebrew funeral chant. It was one of the saddest refrains I had ever heard. None of us dared look at the others.

CHAPTER ELEVEN
"There is Nothing Ahead But Happiness"

Our crew was sent on a one-week rest leave in Hawaii. Still stunned, we flew back in a comfortable Navy Douglas C-54 passenger plane. Seated close together on the long flight, we did not discuss what had happened. We dealt with our emotions by avoiding the incident altogether. Just as it was an unwritten rule not to question Captain Heath, so it was that we did not revisit our experience. We were glad to be alive.

The enlisted men chose to stay at a rest camp on Waikiki Beach as the officers went on to another island. The camp consisted of a single, one-story building. There were rows of double-bunk beds on each side of a lone aisle, a small dining hall at one end, and a paddleball court at the other. The famous beach was a few steps away. As soon as we could, we bought patterned Hawaiian sports shirts and wore them every day. We swam, played paddleball, sprayed golf balls all over the nearby municipal course, and watched the "Hawaii Calls" radio show being broadcast back to the States from the steps of the Mauna Loa hotel. And we loafed in the warm sun on the warm sand. Guam and the war were far behind us.

It was at Waikiki that innocence struck again. Two young women from the States who were working on the island dropped by our camp, which offered a good beach front and the companionship of young airmen. They approached one day as Jim and I were playing paddleball and struck up a conversation. They returned the next day to swim, and we walked with them in the Waikiki area. One was an attractive blond from Hollywood, Florida. She invited me to go dancing one night on a crowded warehouse floor. As we shuffled about the packed room, her fingers lightly brushed the back of my neck. She moved closer and casually mentioned that, in her opinion, if a man and a woman were attracted to each other — and were discreet — they could have sexual relations and no one would be the wiser. I thought that was an interesting observation, but said nothing. Seated in the barracks back in Guam a week later, I suddenly realized what she had suggested.

Stacks of mail awaited our return. This time I opened one of Bake's letters first. Her first line told me how sorry she was to hear about my father's death. A letter from Bill gave the details. Dad had attended a paper makers' union meeting in Glens Falls, then collapsed outside the building. I quickly wrote home, but for some reason did not tell the rest of the crew what had happened. I didn't want to bother them with more sadness, or, more likely, I didn't know how I would behave in the face of their sympathy.

I had forgotten that crew officers censored our mail, so the news soon reached Captain Heath. He and the others were most considerate, and he wrote to Mom. I went through it all numbly, not yet comprehending what had happened.

There was other news. Jim quietly announced that he was not going to fly again. He had gone to see the group's commanding officer, who had given him permission to transfer into an ordinance unit.

"I've had it," Jim said. "They're not going to get me into one of those things again."

"Why, Jim?" I asked. "The war's just about over."

"I just can't do it any more." He had taken enough of the fighting, and had the courage to say so. Part of me could understand his decision, but another part could not. The war was winding down, and it seemed reasonable to me that we should keep on until Japan fell. Jim packed, shook hands all around, and left. I did not see him again until after the end of the war, when he returned to our hut and we exchanged our home addresses.

Not long after that, two Navy officers appeared at our door. One was George Walker's brother. They had come to talk to George's crewmates about what had happened. They asked us questions, but for some reason, we were strangely noncommittal. We gave them short, bland answers, without any hint of blame. We did so

One of the leaflets dropped on Japanese cities late in World War II to warn them in advance of coming bombing raids. This was an effective psychological measure.

either out of loyalty to Captain Heath, or through the same reaction that had kept us from talking among ourselves. I remember being disappointed at my behavior. George's brother was looking for information to comfort him in his loss, or better to explain it, but we could offer little help. All we could say was that George had been a fine person, and that we missed him.

The remainder of our crew resumed flying, with replacements filling in the gaps. By then the B-29 command was dropping leaflets on smaller Japanese cities, listing eleven that would be bombed in the coming week. It was a dramatic psychological move, for there was nothing the enemy could do about it. We went on six such flights, completing twenty-one missions by the time the war came to an end.

We had often wondered during the course of the war why the city of Kyoto had never been bombed. Late in July of 1945 Rea returned excitedly from talking to his friends at group headquarters. He had an explanation.

"Listen to this," he said. "I just heard something interesting over at Group. There's a rumor that we've got something called an 'atom bomb.' It's supposed to be more powerful than any other kind. They plan to try it out on Kyoto."

We were both puzzled and pleased by the news. I was puzzled because I had no idea what an atom bomb was. I remember thinking it might have to do with the atoms in the air and wondered how such an explosion could be limited. What would keep it from going on and on and on? At the same time, I was pleased to think that the new weapon could help hasten an end to the war and send us all back to our homes.

Part of Rea's report was wrong — Kyoto had been spared because it was a religious center. But the rumor about the new weapon was correct. On August 6 the Enola Gay dropped an atomic bomb on Hiroshima. Three days later, a second bomb was detonated above Nagasaki.

The practice of bombing undefended cities that began with a hot air balloon attack on Venice in 1849 had reached its stunning climax nearly a century later over Japan. Two atomic bombs had taken 76,000 lives, had wounded 80,000 others, and obliterated two cities.

It became clear after a time why the atomic bomb had to be employed. The ferocious fights for Saipan, Iwo Jima and Okinawa were grim warnings of the carnage that would follow if Japan itself was invaded. The three battles were essentially prolonged suicides by the defenders. In the spring of 1944 nearly half of the American troops who went ashore at Saipan were killed or wounded. A year later the Marines landed on Iwo Jima for what they thought would be "a brief, but bloody battle" that would last three or four days. Instead, five weeks of bitter fighting were required to take the eight-square-mile island. All but 212 of the 21,000 Iwo Jima defenders fought to the death, while 26,000 American were killed or wounded. The eleven-week Okinawa campaign that began on April 1 of 1945 had been one of the fiercest of the war, killing 7,613 Americans and wounding 31,507. The battle also took the lives of 110,000 Japanese, many of them civilians. And Okinawa was only seventy miles long. All together, the battles of Saipan, Iwo and Okinawa had resulted in 80,000 American casualties and 168,000 Japanese dead.

With a Japanese army of two million men said to be ready to defend the homeland with suicidal ferocity, American military leaders estimated that staggering losses would be incurred in the invasion of the home islands. The estimates ranged from a quarter million casualties to one and a half million. The defenders proclaimed that they would fight on "even if one hundred million die." How long, and at what cost, would it have taken Allied troops to overcome the opposition of men and women prepared to give their lives to their emperor?

"I just wish they had dropped the thing long before they did," Chuck Eagle said after the war. "I saw them bringing back truckloads of dead GIs on Saipan. The bomb couldn't have come soon enough to suit me."

Most of the attention has been paid to the losses that would have been suffered by the ground troops during the landings in Japan and the furious rear-guard actions that would have followed. But the hated B-29s had destroyed every Japanese city with a population of 60,000 or more and had killed hundreds of thousands of people. With thousands of Japanese fighter planes and kamikazes being held in reserve in special suicide units, it is quite possible that entire Superfortress squadrons could have been rammed in an aerial Armageddon during Japan's final hours. Those lucky enough to bail out of crippled bombers could expect to be brutally treated upon landing. And what would have happened to the thousands of prisoners of war being held in Japanese camps? They would have received little mercy. Sixty-two captured B-29 airmen perished in a Tokyo prison during the May 25 fire raid after their captors apparently refused to release them as flames neared.

There are those who argue that Japan would have surrendered if the bomb had not been dropped. They point out that the nation was being pounded relentlessly by sea and air and could not have held out much longer. They argue that our warships could have stood offshore, our aircraft could have continued their attacks, and the Japanese could have been starved into submission. Such a scenario overlooks a number of points. One is that the Navy took more losses from 1,900 Kamikaze attacks off Okinawa than it did at Pearl Harbor, and that the Japanese still had many more suicide planes and pilots hidden in reserve. They could have attacked under the cover of darkness. Another is that numerous Japanese strongholds — less dear than the home islands themselves — had been heavily bombed and shelled in the march across the Pacific, but they had not surrendered without costly Army and Marine landings. They had been fanatically defended. A third point is that the Japanese Diet had voted, 3-3, not to surrender even after the second atomic bomb had been dropped.

So it is quite likely that Japan would have fought on for some time if the atomic bomb had not been released. We will never know how long that might have been. The invasion of Kyushu, the southernmost Japanese home island, was set for November 1 of 1945 and the landings on Honshu, the main island, for the following spring. Untold thousands of Americans would have been added to the casualty lists in those campaigns. Our leaders therefore made a cruel choice between the immediate loss of additional Japanese civilians and the inevitable loss of more U.S. soldiers, marines, sailors and airmen.

How callous of those who argue today that the atomic bomb should not have been dropped because the Allied invasion casualty estimates had been exaggerated — that "only" 50,000 to 95,000 members of the landing forces would have become casualties rather than the higher estimates. Far more Japanese would have died, as well; if the Okinawa campaign was a guideline, 110,000 Japanese would perish for every 7,000 Allied invaders.

The atomic bomb was a terrible weapon, but so were the thousands of incendiary bombs that had turned Japanese and German cities into infernos during the war. The first fire raid on Tokyo in March of 1945 burned at 1,800 degrees and took more lives than did the Hiroshima bomb. The British RAF raids on German cities had suffocated and incinerated thousands of civilians during the war, and the Germans in turn had sent V-1 and V-2 bombs winging indiscriminately toward London. In the cold calculus of war, the atomic bomb was simply a new, more efficient way to beat an enemy into submission.

Some historians contend that Hiroshima should not have been bombed because it had been U.S. policy "to spare noncombatants." B-29 crews knew of no such restriction. Indeed, the opposite was the case: Japanese cities were deliberately burned to the ground to help end that nation's resistance. The same policy had been pursued by both Allied and Axis forces throughout the war and had resulted in the devastation of Warsaw, Rotterdam, London, Berlin, Hamburg, Leningrad, Coventry, Dresden, Cologne,

Tokyo, Nagoya, Osaka and other major cities. The precedent of annihilating populations had been set long before Hiroshima and Nagasaki. "The unimaginable had become acceptable," as one writer has noted. Wars have a way of doing that. Enemies become dehumanized, be they German or Japanese. Remember if you will that sentence from the *New York Times'* account of our April 13 fire raid on Tokyo: "The sight of the capitol aflame would thrill any American..."

Long after the end of the war, former President Dwight D. Eisenhower stated that the bomb should not have been employed. In short, we should have accepted the additional casualties that would have resulted if the war had been pursued in traditional ways. Possibly so, but one wonders what former General Dwight D. Eisenhower might have said if, while serving as the Supreme Commander of the Allied forces preparing to invade Europe in 1944, he had been told that an atomic bomb dropped on Berlin could have saved the hundreds of thousands of casualties that lay ahead in the Normandy landings, the Battle of the Bulge, and the drive into Germany. Normandy alone claimed 225,000 Allied casualties and 200,000 Germans. The atomic bomb had not been developed at that time, but the question is an intriguing one.

Writing long after the horrifying effects of radioactivity had become known, modern-day historians enjoy "the lucid view that hindsight affords." At the time the atomic bomb was dropped, the majority of American— and certainly all the fighting men I knew— approved its use.

Even so, I wondered in August of 1945 why the atomic bomb could not have been detonated elsewhere first as a warning. Why not in Japan's inland sea or off-shore, where the force of the bomb could have been shown without such terrible loss of life? Apparently our leaders felt that a demonstration might fail or might not be enough to convince the Japanese. Perhaps, too, they wanted to impress the Soviet Union, which then controlled half of Europe, had taken Manchuria in the final weeks of the war, and undoubtedly would be pleased to see the United States and Japan slugging it out for additional months.

On August 14, the base PA system clicked to life again. "Attention, everyone: here's what we've been waiting for. It's all over. Japan has surrendered." A scrawled sign quickly appeared on the group bulletin board : "THE WAR IS OVER!!" We looked at each other and shook hands. We were relieved, yet felt somewhat at a loss with no more missions to prepare for.

There were two more long flights to come. On September 2 every bomber that could take to the air flew to Japan, where the formal surrender was to take place aboard the U.S.S. Missouri in Tokyo Bay. We flew up the coast northeast of the Bay, turned inland, overflew the ceremony in a long parade, banked back north, and repeated the process. To the Japanese it appeared that there were twice as many B-29s as was the case. We gazed down on history in the making: a lethal-looking fleet of gray warships covering the bay as General Douglas MacArthur and Japanese officials signed the final documents. World War II was officially ended.

For the first time in history, air power alone had forced a nation into submission. Even before the atomic bombs had been dropped, the B-29s had burned out 150 square miles in sixty-five cities, and had destroyed 83% of Japan's oil production and 73% of her aircraft production.

General James Doolittle, who led the symbolic B-25 raid on Tokyo from the aircraft carrier Hornet in 1942, noted after the war that "The Navy had the transport to make invasion possible; the ground forces had the power to make it possible; the B-29 made it unnecessary."

A few weeks later, a similar show of strength carried us to the east coast of Korea. We flew across the peninsula, just below the parallel separating the two halves of the country. The goal apparently was to impress the North Koreans. They were not awed: five years later, they stormed into South Korea.

We began the long wait to go home. September, October and November dragged by. We spent our time building an enlisted men's club, playing basketball, and flying enough hours to earn our monthly flight pay. We often took a few Army engineers on the flights to reward them for building our base. I sat in the right blister position one day on a ride that carried us around the island of Guam for a few hours. Three black soldiers sat on the deck close by. When it came time to land, I called out the gear and flap positions and watched the jungle and landing strip come closer. We dropped lower and lower. Suddenly, the pilot poured power into the engines and began retracting the wheels and flaps to go around for another landing. But we continued sagging; the pavement seemed only a few feet below, and was inching closer. I expected us to hear the screech of metal striking asphalt any second to start us on a terrifying half-mile slide.

"Christ," I thought, "we made it through the war, and now this." I looked about the cabin, and saw the flash of teeth among our smiling passengers. They were unaware of what was happening.

After agonizing moments, we pulled up and circled around the field for our landing. I did not know what had happened to cause our pilot or co-pilot to abort the landing. Possibly we were too far along the runway for safety. My heart was still thumping as we taxied to our hardstand and began working our way out of the plane. One of the engineers turned to me to shake hands.

"Thanks for the ride," he said. "That sure was fun when we buzzed the field that time."

A devastating typhoon struck Okinawa, so a fleet of B-29s loaded up with tents and supplies for the island. As was so often the case when dozens of bombers were in the air any length of time, with or without opposition, one of them had trouble and ditched at sea. That sent us out a day later on search missions, dividing hundreds of miles of glaring ocean into grids to be scanned on long afternoons. It was tedious duty. We had to keep reminding ourselves that somewhere down there men in life rafts were counting on us.

Most of all, we wondered when we could go home. Although we had been overseas only eight months, we became obsessed with the idea of flying back for Christmas. A list would come out every week with the names of those scheduled to return, and we examined it carefully to see if anyone on it was less deserving.

The order of return was determined by the number of points accumulated through missions flown, medals earned, and time overseas. Fortunately, we had won air medals and had twenty-one missions to our credit. In addition, each of us had been awarded a Purple Heart medal because of the "scrapes and immersion" we suffered in our bail-out. I was not proud of that; Rea had obtained the medals through his contacts at Group, and I never thought we deserved them. Our "wounds" were trivial compared with the grievous injuries that others received during the war.

Nevertheless, it all added up to enough points to start Ken, Rea and me back late in November. On Thanksgiving Day — the perfect date — we feasted on turkey, bid farewell to the other gunners, and boarded a B-29. We flew across the International Date Line to

Hawaii, where it still was Thanksgiving and time for more turkey.

There was one final scare. I was listening to the strange pilot and engineer as we approached Hawaii and heard them talking about the fuel situation. We were low on gas and would have to fly straight into Roger's Field without an approach pattern. "Not again," I thought, but we landed safely.

Another flight carried us to Sacramento on November 28. There we climbed down from a B-29 for the last time. We turned in our flight equipment and checked into a barracks. The next day, a bus took us to Camp Stoneman, across the bay from San Francisco. We waited a rainy week for a troop train to carry us east. Our destination was Ft. Dix, where it all had begun nearly two years before.

Upon our arrival we unloaded, handed in the rest of our gear, and waited for our discharge papers to be processed. There was a small airfield at the base. I wandered over one day and saw a strange sight: an airplane with no propeller. There was a large hole in the front, and a roar came out the rear. The plane looked small and feeble as it took off, powered by something called a jet engine. Clearly, I thought, it was an experiment that bore little promise.

My discharge came through on December 13. With $182.30 in back pay and severance money in my pocket, I made my way to New York city, where I caught the train to Albany. I looked out on the frozen, moonlit Hudson River as we sped north. I felt happy, proud and satisfied in my Air Force uniform. The war was over and I was safely on my way home. A young girl sat next to me, reading sheet music, chewing gum, and humming to herself. She was oblivious of the be-ribboned soldiers and sailors all about her. What different lives we lead, I thought.

The last bus had left Albany, and the Delaware and Hudson train to Ft. Edward did not run at night. I wandered around Union Station or tried to nap on the hard benches. The next morning, my train was chugging back up the Hudson valley.

It was a brisk, clear winter day. The ground was covered with fresh snow. The sunlight dazzled my eyes. I caught the bus to Hudson Falls, got off at Maple Street, and walked home again. I didn't know whether to ring the bell or go straight in. I rang the bell, and Mom opened the door. She brightened when she saw me.

"I'm so happy," she said, opening her arms. "You're finally home." There were tears in her eyes. "How I wish your father were here to see you now."

"So do I."

I entered the house and looked around the room. The house seemed quite empty. My cousin Ruth was at work, and her husband and Chuck had yet to return from Europe. A picture of Dad stood on a table. Nearby was the big chair in which he had sat, with its ever-present ash tray stand.

"I'm sorry about Dad," I said.

"I know. But he didn't suffer. It was over so quickly. He went off to the meeting with Bill and never came back." She looked older and sadder.

"Your father read about the war every day, and wondered about you and Charles."

"Did he worry about us?"

"Yes. When you wrote from Hawaii that you had scraped your leg when you jumped out of your airplane, he said he thought you had lost a leg, and were keeping that from us."

"What a shame," I said. "I was perfectly okay. I hope that had nothing to do with his heart attack."

"I don't think it did. He hadn't been at all well for a long time. You remember the nitroglycerin pills he had to take."

"I knew he had angina, but I didn't realize how serious it was."

I carried my bag to a small upstairs bedroom and looked around. In a closet were hangers that held the Hart, Schaefner and Marx suit that I had sent home from Fort Dix, and my football letter jacket. I tried the jacket on.

After I unpacked, I called Bake.

"Hi," I said. "Guess what - I'm here."

"Welcome home."

"When can I see you?"

"Can you come over for dinner tonight?"

"I'd better not. I'll stay here with Mom and Ruth for a while. But I'll be by right after that."

That evening I walked excitedly over to Mechanic Street and onto the familiar long porch of the gray-brick Baker home. Bake answered the door bell. She looked pretty in her heavy sweater, skirt, and loafers. We did not fly into each other's arms, for that was not our way.

"Home at last," she said. "It's been a while."

"Almost two years. This is wonderful." I looked around the warm front room and at our big blue chair. "Thanks for all those letters, Bake. I loved getting them. They really helped." Suddenly the words came out: "You know what — you look like someone from a magazine. You look beautiful." I could not get over my good fortune.

Mrs. Baker came out of the kitchen with a smile.

"Well, look who's here," she said. "How nice to have you home again."

"It feels great. I still can't believe it."

"I hate to think of what that young man has been through," she said, looking at Bake while referring to me.

"It wasn't all that bad, really."

After a time, Bake suggested that we go out for a walk. I quickly agreed. Both of us wanted to be alone. She put on her tan coat, scarf, ear muffs and mittens, and we covered the several blocks to her father's drugstore. She brought me up to date on what had been happening in Hudson Falls, but we did not talk about my overseas experiences.

Late that night, back in her parlor, we ate ice cream and talked with her parents. As Bake and her mother washed the dishes, Harry Baker started down the stairs to the cellar with his coal bucket. I offered to help, but he declined. He was a proud man. He shoveled coal into the bucket from the large bin and returned, puffing after his climb. He banked over the fire for the night in the big iron kitchen stove. Then he and his wife turned in.

"Good night, Andy ," she said. "I'm glad you're safely back."

Bake and I quickly settled into our blue chair. She looked up at me.

"So am I," she said.

Remaining with me still are Ken Cox's words the day we landed in California in November of 1945. Ken and Rea and I were waiting for transportation to our quarters. As we stood there, Ken turned and said "You know, there is nothing ahead of us but happiness." That was true; the war was behind us, and we had only to return to our families and friends and get on with our lives. It was beautiful thought.

Bake and Andy in 1995.

Forty-five years later: the author and Jim Dudley in Tampa, Florida in 1990.

CHAPTER TWELVE
Fifty Years Later

Half a century after the end of the war, many of the details of our experiences have long since faded, while others remain as vivid as the day they took place.

What happened to our old crew? Rea Schuessler and I corresponded for several years. He became the director of the municipal stadium at Mobile, Alabama, where he staged the annual Senior Bowl football game between graduating college players from the North and South. He died of cancer several years ago.

I lost track of Jim Dudley until 1986, when I wrote to the College Park newspaper to ask if any readers knew his whereabouts. A woman replied that he lived in Tampa, Florida. I called Jim, and we talked excitedly. He had retired after working as a customer services manager of two airlines. He had been married three times and had three sons by his first wife. One son had been given my full name, Andrew Meredith, which was quite gratifying.

I visited the Dudleys in 1990. We met at the airport, where Jim and I finally recognized each other and embraced warmly. We had a fine reunion, talking far into the night about our adventures. He recalled another detail that I had forgotten, or had not known: that he and Rea Schuessler had spent the night of our bail-out half-submerged in a one-man life raft after one of their rafts had failed to open.

It was then that Jim told me how Lieutenant O'Brien had gone down with our bomber rather than parachute into the sea. I was astounded at the news — and even more so by the fact that I had not been aware of what had happened. How could I have been so oblivious? How much more have I missed throughout my life by not being more attentive?

Jim has retained his soft Georgian drawl, has a strong, quiet character, and clearly is highly regarded at his golf club, which we visited. The youngster I knew could still be glimpsed in that bespectacled, sixty-five-year-old figure. I felt a sense of completion, having tracked down my closest friend from those incredible two years of our youth.

All of the others have disappeared. Captain Heath died from a rare disease in South America after the war. Ken Cox, Abe Veroba and Herb Kestenbaum were from large cities, so it is impossible to trace them. Paul Klenk and Chuck Mienke are only memories.

When I returned home in December of 1945 it was clear that the world longed to return to normal. The war had broken out, it had caught up the young men of our village, and now most of us were coming back. Our return was taken almost as a matter of course by those who had gone and by those who had remained behind. There were no big parties and no parades; the men simply filtered back into town. I did not buy GI life insurance when I was discharged, and did not join the American Legion or the Veterans of Foreign Wars. I wanted the break to be complete. I took off my uniform, hung it up in a closet, and never saw it again.

I was eligible for "52-20 club" payments — twenty dollars a week from the government for a year. I drew a few checks, then got a job as a laborer in a construction company. A few months later, Bake surprised me with the news that she was planning to go away to college in the fall. I didn't know what to think; I had somehow expected life to go on as it was and had not given college a thought. Higher education seemed well beyond my means and background. But the GI Bill of Rights — the Servicemen's Readjustment Act of 1944 — opened a wide door for me. The act provided qualified servicemen with four years of college. It covered tuition, fees, books and supplies, and a subsistence allowance of $50 a month. I decided to look into it.

I visited our old high school and was given permission to use a classroom typewriter at night to write to universities for information. On the recommendation of our high school principal, I applied to St. Lawrence University, a small coeducational school on the northern border of New York. I was accepted, as were many other former servicemen. Far more of us showed up the first week than the University expected, so some of us were assigned to bunk beds that were hurriedly set up in the vacated girl's locker room of a gymnasium.

At St. Lawrence I plunged immediately into the realm of seventeen-year-old freshmen. I felt that theirs was the real world, and that we older veterans were interlopers who had to adjust to it. Thirteen months before, I had been wearing a flak helmet over Japan and writing letters home about the war; now I wore a frosh beanie and composed earnest English 101 essays about my impressions of the campus. On our dates we talked about our classes, professors, exams, and the alumni homecoming displays being prepared by the fraternities and sororities. The veterans I knew did not dwell on the conflict, nor write about it. The present and future were far more important than the past. Our experiences were behind us; we had gone from boyhood to battle and back to boyhood.

As the only one in our family to attend college, I felt that I should concentrate on my studies. I did not try out for the football team. I began writing instead for the school newspaper and magazine, the newsletter of the fraternity I joined, and for the college publicity office as a volunteer.

I soon found that there are those in the world who are proficient with numbers and those who are more comfortable with words. I was not one of the numbers people. I enrolled in a pre-engineering program, but had little interest in measuring the velocity of balls rolling down an inclined plane, and failed utterly to understand how calculus could determine the volume of a cylinder. After a few months, I switched to majors in English and history, my true interests.

I was graduated in 1950. At a cost of only $5.5 billion, the GI Bill eventually produced 450,000 engineers, 240,000 accountants, 238,000 teachers, 91,000 scientists, 67,000 doctors, 22,000 dentists, 17,000 writers and editors, and thousands of other professionals. That investment in the nation's veterans was repaid hundreds of times over in only a few decades through increased productivity and higher taxes. It was an enlightened piece of legislation that played a critical role in America's astounding postwar economic growth.

Bake and I first went in opposite directions. She enrolled at Briarcliff Junior College in southern New York and later transferred to Bryant College in Providence, Rhode Island. Her schools were hundreds of miles southeast of Hudson Falls; my school lay hundreds of miles to the northwest. But our long correspondence continued throughout our college years. We met when I could hitch-hike across three states to Providence and when we came home for holidays and summer vacations. We were married in July of 1950, a month after I graduated from St. Lawrence. We have three fine daughters, Susan, Ann and Nancy, and two grand-daughters, Meredith and Rebecca.

I did not have to follow my father and siblings into the mills, after all. My writing activities in college led to a job as a newspaper reporter for the *Watertown Times*. After earning $2,500 a year for two years as the one-man *Times* bureau correspondent at Canton — the St. Lawrence County seat and home of the University — I entered the college public relations field at Johns Hopkins University. Although I had steered clear of engineering classes while in college, I became fascinated by the scientific research being conducted by the Hopkins faculty. That interest led in turn to a job at the University of Michigan as science and engineering editor.

We were in Ann Arbor from 1954 to 1963. It was a time of intense national interest in technical news, particularly after the Soviets launched their Sputnik in 1959. I enjoyed the challenge of reporting scientific achievements in a way that the researcher found fair and accurate and readers found understandable.

In 1963, I joined the staff of Stanford University, where I handled general public relations duties until being named Director of Community Relations in 1972. I served in that capacity until my retirement in 1993.

My brother Chuck returned home a month after I did, lean and leathery. He had entered the war in southwestern Germany and had lugged a heavy Browning Automatic Rifle in the drive across the nation to Linz, Austria. He had used it often. He carried with him the SS insignia that he had ripped from the lapel of a fallen German soldier. Chuck also worked on construction jobs after the war, then followed his bent: electricity. He eventually became head electrician at the Finch, Prynn Paper Company in Glens Falls, where he could be depended upon to roll out of bed at any time of the night to respond to an electrical problem at the mill. Like my father and brother Bill, Chuck smoked cigarettes continually. All three died before they reached sixty years of age. Chuck's wife has also died; their children, Chip and Hope, live in the Glens Falls area. He is the last male Doty on our portion of the family tree.

Only three other members of my family remain: Ruth, a widow in Mechanicville, N.Y.; Betty, a widow in Florida; and Ann, who lives with her husband in Sackett's Harbor, N.Y. My mother, Ken Howe, Agnes and Leah all have passed on, as have Bake's parents.

All the members of our old gang survived the war, thanks to their relatively late entrance into the conflict. Bob Burns served as the best man at our wedding. Chuck Eagle married Peg McGinnis, and they now live in Hudson Falls. Jim Fraser and the former Claire Carleton reside at Lake George. Gerry Ellsworth, the boy who saw me off that frosty morning in 1944, is in retirement in North Carolina. I've lost track of "Irish Bill" DeCamillo and "McGoosey" Walsh. Bud Reed, one of the greatest hell-raisers in our gang, eventually became the principal of a local high school.

CHAPTER THIRTEEN
"OUR HEARTS WERE TOUCHED BY FIRE"

Gentlemen now abed in England will think themselves accurs'd they were not here.
— Henry V to his soldiers before the Battle of Agincourt in 1415, according to Shakespeare

This memoir would not be complete if it did not place my experiences, my generation, and World War II in perspective. What was clear in 1945, and is even clearer today, is that I was extremely lucky. I was among the small percentage of men who come under enemy fire in a war, but I did not see the worst of it. I was a latecomer into military service, into the B-29 program, and into combat. Had I been born a year earlier, or entered service earlier, I could have undergone far more hazardous times over Europe or Japan, or in another branch of the armed forces.

Our bomber crew experienced some difficult moments, yet we did not suffer the periods of sustained terror or hardship that others encountered during the war. The men who struggled in the jungles of Guadalcanal or Burma, shivered in winter foxholes, underwent daily Kamikaze attacks aboard their ships, battled their way the length of Okinawa or crossed freezing Italian rivers in the face of intense enemy fire, faced war at its worst.

War is such a game of chance. Those who turn eighteen at the outset of a conflict have far less chance of emerging unscathed than their younger colleagues. So do those who find themselves in the first waves of a bitterly-contested amphibious landing or who fly bombing missions when the enemy is at full strength. How many of the Royal Air Force pilots who fought in the Battle of Britain in 1941 were alive at war's end? How many crewmen survived from the first handful of U. S. Eighth Air Force squadrons that flew from England into Germany?

A young man — a boy, actually — could be assigned to an infantry division, where 70% of the casualties were suffered in World War II. After six weeks of fighting in Normandy, all of the original officers and enlisted men in one American division had been killed, wounded, or captured. The stateside "Replacement Centers" had been aptly named.

But if a serviceman were more fortunate he could find himself among the thousands of support personnel who operated behind the lines. The "teeth to tail" ratio of the Army was legendary, with twenty-seven men needed to sustain one infantryman. A famous *LIFE Magazine* photograph was staged in front of a B-17 bomber. In the first row was the eleven-man crew; ranged behind it were deep ranks of support personnel and equipment. Twelve thousand men were needed at our air base on Guam to keep the 314th Wing's 180 bombers and two thousand crew members in the air. Of all the men who served during the war, only 27% came under enemy fire.

Earlier I noted the importance of the three-month difference between my eighteenth birthday in October of 1943 and my graduation from high school the following January. I was scheduled to graduate in June of 1943, but lost half a year after our family moved to Hudson Falls when I was eleven. Had I graduated in June on schedule I would have been inducted into service that October rather than the following January. Such a timetable might well have found me serving as a ball turret gunner in a B-17 or B-24 over Europe early in 1944, rather than as a B-29 tail gunner over Japan a year later.

The implications of that are profound. The beginning of 1944 saw a thousand German fighter planes and the deadliest antiaircraft fire in the world blasting American bombers from the sky. The Eighth Air Force had resumed its long-range bombing missions in the fall of 1943, thanks to fighter escorts that could fly deep into Germany with their new auxiliary "drop tanks" of fuel, but the duty was still risky. German aircraft were superior to those of the Japanese, and their pilots were highly skilled and aggressive. The air war reached a "fierce crescendo" early that year.

With the Normandy invasion set for June, the Eighth, Ninth and Fifteenth Air Forces in England and Italy had been ordered to drive the Luftwaffe from the sky, prepare the way for the landings, and destroy Germany's factories. In the first nine weeks of that year, 271 B-17s and B-24s were shot down.

The Fifteenth, flying out of Italy, lost a third of its strength in the month of July alone. I could easily have been aboard one of those B-24s or B-17s.

Lady Luck came into play even then, for the B-24 in which I had trained flew lower, more slowly, and in looser formation than the B-17. It presented a more attractive target to German fighters. "Who needs fighter cover when there are B-24s around?" a B-17 gunner once asked.

The Eighth Air Force alone lost a total of 3,900 planes in its three years of combat. Only the infantry suffered a higher casualty rate than the heavy bomber crews over Europe. During the early years, only one crew in four was able to complete a tour of twenty-five missions. One of the handsome young gunners we had seen returning to Hudson Falls in the autumn of 1943 was killed, and the other was wounded and taken prisoner.

As I read today about those terrible early missions — bombers assembling in the clouds above England, men wearing oxygen masks in the bitter cold for hours on end, planes holding in tight formation through fields of flak, gunners fighting off dozens of aggressive attacks, crewmen killed or wounded, bombers exploding and falling in flames, I am filled with admiration — and am grateful that none of those fates befell me. I ask myself how I would have behaved under those brutal conditions. I suspect that I would have quietly accepted my lot.

By contrast, the 20th Air Force lost only 485 B-29s in a year of missions against Japan, relatively few of them through enemy action. The raids had become easier as time passed. Every month of delay had made our lives that much safer. I had fired at only two fighters and saw no B-29s downed by the enemy. We had often been frightened, but never seriously hit. The odds we faced over Japan were far more favorable than those over Europe.

And yet the 20th Air Force counted 3,041 men killed, wounded or missing. The 485 B-29s that were lost were more than 12% of all those built — not all of which went overseas, and many of which arrived in the last months of the war. More than 2,700 B-29s were damaged. I saw five of them destroyed — at Cuba, Iwo Jima, Guam and Saipan, and our own — at a cost of twenty-three men. Our group lost twenty-five airplanes and seventeen crews. George Walker, Donald Hutchison and Richard O'Brien are just as dead as if they had been hit over Stuttgart or Ploesti or Berlin.

Our crew could have been in one of the B-29s that exploded on take-off, or disappeared after ditching at sea. Others flipped upside down in fire raid updrafts, were rammed over the target, were riddled by bullets and flak, or crashed while landing. I could have been the trapped tail gunner whose frozen hands had to be amputated after his compartment was blown open, or the one who fired furiously at an attacking Baka suicide plane until it smashed into the bomber and destroyed everyone. If the pilot of that Irving fighter had been able to slip up on us undetected, he could have blasted us from the sky.

Men exactly like us were in those other planes. The black-bordered photos of lost crews posing in front of their bombers show smiling youths just as we were, officers in the rear row, enlisted men kneeling on one knee in the front, just as we did. In a sense, we are living their lives today; they are what might have happened to us.

Why do men do it? I have long been intrigued by that timeless question. Why are so many willing to risk their lives again and again, often in the face of heavy odds?

There are many answers. To begin with, our generation had no real choice. The nation had been attacked, and war had been declared. All able-bodied men — and thousands of women — were expected to take up arms or join in the cause in other ways. There was no debate.

We fought in a "good" war. Pearl Harbor had been bombed, frontiers had been breached, despots were on the march. The conflict was clear-cut, black and white, obvious good against obvious evil. I knew no one who questioned the merits of the war, and only 5% of draft-age men attempted to avoid service. Men left home sadly and reluctantly, of course, but in general they felt that they were protecting their country, avenging a wrong, and rescuing others from oppression. They were preserving the Four Freedoms enumerated by President Roosevelt and Winston Churchill: freedom of speech and religion, and freedom from want and fear.

"For the first time in my life," one bomber crew member said, "I was doing something important." I felt much the same way.

My generation was patriotic, brought up on the likes of Ethan Allen, John Paul Jones, the Rough Riders, Admiral Farragut and Sergeant York. We sang "There's a Star-Spangled Banner Waving Somewhere," and "It's a Grand Old Flag, it's a high-flying flag... it's the emblem of the land we love, the home of the free and the brave." We believed that our nation was basically good and that our leaders were wise and well-meaning.

We accepted our lot. Acceptance and innocence were the by-words of our era. We did not question what was asked of us. Amazing as that may sound today, we tended to believe what we were told by our elders, by our government, and by organizations of all kinds. We were born thirty years before the wave of self-centered individualism and distrust that swept over America in the 1960s.

The Testosterone Factor surely plays a part. Our task not only was important, it was exciting, as well. We were young men fascinated by the prospect of adventure and combat. We grew up playing with toy guns, sling-shots, sticks that flung rubber bands. "Bang! Bang!" is one of the first cries of a boy at play. Aggressive responses were built into our genes.

I sometimes think that the youth of America — even those of the rest of the world — may actually miss war today, or the possibility of it. With Cold War tensions ended, can it be that the need of young men to take risks and show courage is being met in other ways? Can the growing popularity of rock-climbing, hang-gliding, bungee-jumping, parachuting, kayaking on wild rivers and other dangerous activities be explained by that drive? Could it underlie the appeal of graphic violence in films and television, of gang warfare, or of the fighting that flares among young football and soccer fans?

At this writing, thirty-six major armed conflicts — those that have claimed the lives of a thousand or more people each — are in progress somewhere around the world. National, religious, tribal and ethnic disagreements obviously are major forces in those clashes, but could testosterone also be at work?

Lastly, there is a motivation that goes well beyond patriotism and combative instincts. It is what others may think. One's reputation was at stake — in his home town, in his squadron, in his bomber. A crewman could not let down his comrades nor appear to be "yellow." I don't remember anyone on our crew expressing fear, although I could sense it through the total silence on the intercom on take-offs, landings and bomb runs. The rare crew that aborted too many missions, or that dumped its bombs just off-target to avoid the worst opposition in a night raid, raised eyebrows. We were all in it together, and no one should shirk.

Throughout history, pride and the fear of peer disapproval have helped drive untold thousands of men against the swords, pikes, crossbows, guns and artillery of their enemies. The Light Brigade at Balaklava, Pickett's Confederate troops at Cemetery Ridge, the British at Ypres, the Marines at Tarawa, the Rangers at Pont du Hoc, the Navy pilots at Midway, the submarine crews in the Pacific could not allow themselves to be cowardly or fail to carry their share of the load.

Some modern authors argue that World War II was not at all "good." They point out that the conflict was so thoroughly mythologized, sanitized and Hollywoodized that we fail to realize its true horror and absurdity. They describe the terror, carnage and atrocities that were never reported back home; the youth and naiveté of the men who took up arms; the inferiority of some American equipment; the racism that prevailed; the petty "chicken shit" that was encountered in the military.

Almost gleefully, it seems, they detail the stupid mistakes that were made, the propaganda that flowed, the men and material wasted, the regimentation that took place, the sheer insanity of it all — even the widespread use of alcohol and profanity among servicemen. They like to observe that more soldiers suffered from venereal disease in the Italian campaign than were wounded in combat.

All of this may be true and cannot be ignored. War is indeed an obscene way to settle disputes, and terrible and stupid things do happen in the pursuit of victory. World War II was no exception. But at least that conflict had an aura about it that few wars have had. Many of us entered it with high ideals, viewed it as a noble crusade, and prefer to remember it that way.

The revisionist authors argue that their goal is simply to remind us of the folly of war and to warn the nation against the easy overreliance on arms in the future. That may true, but I think they may also derive satisfaction from showing that their moral standards are higher than those of others. In the name of scholarship they can portray institutions and individuals as evil, and thus define themselves as good.

The modern-day critics — many of them born since the end of the war — run the risk of denigrating what so many men and women did in the name of their cause fifty years ago. Sixteen million Americans gave years of their lives — and many their entire lives — to set the world right and insure a better future. They did what they thought was right.

How do men deal with the awful reality that their lives could end in an instant or that they could be forever crippled? They do it through innocence, self-delusion, bravado, optimism and prayer. As suggested earlier, young men are under the impression that life stretches on for decade after decade, that they are indestructible, and that the worst will befall "the other guys." They have faith that they will survive, and they call often on a Higher Power to bring that about. They dare not think otherwise. I sent my parents a Christmas card from Pyote in 1944. It bore the picture of a B-29 among fluffy clouds. Beneath it I had written: "Don't worry, I'll be back." I had no doubt that I would.

Just as the war itself may be viewed through a different lens today, so can the attitudes of the men who fought in it. Modern observers may regard our unquestioning patriotism and obedience as something similar to the behavior of lemmings tumbling blindly after each other into the sea to drown.

The sexual innocence of our era may now be seen as Victorian prudishness; our strong faith in the nation and its leaders, astounding naiveté. Because of our obsession with economic and military security (or because of our lack of resources) we may also be accused of neglecting the environment, tolerating racial discrimination, and allowing corporations the freedom to do much as they pleased. But we did the best we could with the cards we were dealt, given the temper of our times.

We held also to an old-fashioned notion that individuals were responsible for their own actions. We find it hard today to understand why those who fail to prevent others from being reckless or foolish are being held accountable. Our simple ethic demanded that young men resolve their differences through one-on-one fisticuffs rather than through the use of knives, pistols, AK-47s, gang-stompings, and drive-by shootings.

Our strict teachers could be the subject today of parental ire, school board reprimands or even legal action. Men taught not to swear in the presence of women still squirm a bit in modern movie houses and theaters when the air is filled with a steady stream of profanity.

Although many of those old values may now cause younger heads to shake in wonderment, I think we were the better for them. We enjoyed innocent childhoods that extended well into our teens, if not through them; we took pride in our nation; we trusted others; we embraced standards that were simple, rewarding, and reassuring. We felt safer.

Combat is not without its personal rewards. The experience taught me early in life that I could cope with difficult situations. It instilled in me a sense of pride and a personal philosophy that has lasted a lifetime — the realization that the ultimate deadline is death, and that anything short of that can be dealt with much easier. The war made possible a college education that I never would have otherwise attained — which in turn opened the way to a productive and fulfilling career, and early home ownership.

Finally, most of us were fortunate in other important ways, even though we had been enveloped in the greatest war of all time. In the decades that followed the conflagration, we participated in a national economic boom that was the envy of the world. We were able to attend college at low cost, find jobs fairly easily, feel secure in our work, and be virtually assured career advancements if we performed halfway well. We purchased homes at low rates of interest for tens of thousands of dollars and watched the property steadily increase in value. A new car could be obtained for the price of some of today's monthly mortgage payments. Most of our wives did not have to work, staying home with children instead — children we later sent to college at a fraction of today's tuition. Baby-sitters were available at fifty cents and hour. Our offspring are filled with envy when they hear of our good fortune.

This section opened with that memorable quotation from Shakespeare: "And gentlemen in England now abed shall think themselves accurs'd they were not here." He was right, as he so often was. Those who emerge alive and whole from combat share a camaraderie, a quiet pride, a sense of good fortune, that few others enjoy. It is a feeling that seems to intensify over the years; it is one that can make old veterans insufferable if they are not careful.

After the Civil War, Oliver Wendell Holmes Jr. wrote: "We have shared the incommunicable experience of war. We have felt, we still feel, the passion of life to its top... In our youths, our hearts were touched by fire."

Martin van Creveld, a military historian at Hebrew University in Jerusalem, said it this way: "Throughout history, for every person who has expressed his horror of war there is another who found in it the most marvelous of all experiences that are vouchsafed to man, even to the point that he later spent a lifetime boring his descendants by recounting his exploits."

Amen. Yet those veterans should be forgiven if they look back over their shoulders now and then. Many of them encountered more danger before they turned twenty or twenty-five than the average person meets in an entire lifetime.

This is the last great hurrah of the World War II generation. The men who took up arms in that conflict participated in one of the monumental events in the history of the world. There is great satisfaction in having served in a "popular" war waged by a united, determined, resourceful nation. There is an inner glow that comes from having been tested, and in having met the test.

Acknowledgments

This all began when our daughters, Susan, Ann and Nancy, began asking about life in the 1930s, about the days when their parents first met, and about "the war." This record is for them and coming generations.

Bake — my good wartime and college correspondent and lifetime companion — holds my affection for her steady support throughout, and for her patience as I immersed myself in the past.

I am most grateful to Pat Brito of Design and Print Services and Roxanna Morales of Graphanalia for their work on this publication, and to Bob Topor for directing me to them. I have relied on their expertise and good taste. Thanks to David Brito for his keen interest and sharp eye.

Many others have helped me. Peter Allen, Stanford University Editor Emeritus, kindly reviewed my manuscript and offered suggestions. So did Pat Westerhouse, an expert on human relations, who provided helpful insights about the people and events reported in this book. Rob Van der Wyngaart, a friend from the Netherlands, offered fine suggestions. His command of English as a second language exceeds my own use of my native tongue.

Chuck Eagle of Hudson Falls quickly responded to my requests for information about the village and about the work of the Sand Hill Iron & Brass Company during the conflict. Chuck also offered his own wartime memories.

Tom Lubesmeyer opened the Boeing Company's photo archives

to me and generously provided prints for my use.

Betsy Roden encouraged me to push ahead with the book, as did Gail Stypula and Pete McCloskey, a former Marine combat officer and U.S. Congressman. Thanks, too, for the interest and encouragement of Vice Admiral James Stockdale of the Hoover Institution at Stanford University, Carroll Harrington of Palo Alto and Ellie Huggins of Truckee, California.

Members of the 19th Bombardment Association, the 20th Air Force Association and the Air Force Gunners Association responded graciously to my requests for information, as did former B-29 pilots Harry Chagnon, Jim Handwerker, Chester Marshall and Vernon Chandler.

Gentle prodding and/or encouragement came from Marilyn Price Mitchell, Phil Williams, Bob Weeks and Peter Smith. My thanks to them all.